A TIME TO PRAY

WITH THE OLD TESTAMENT

Also available from GIA Publications, Inc.:
A Time to Pray: With the New Testament

A Time to Pray: With the Old Testament is
designed for use with:

Journey Through the Old Testament

and *Scripture Study Book: Old Testament*

published by Harcourt Religion Publishers.

A TIME TO PRAY

WITH THE OLD TESTAMENT

PRAYER CELEBRATIONS FOR YOUTH
BY DAVID HAAS

MUSIC BY DAVID HAAS
WITH TONY ALONSO, MICHAEL BALHOFF, JOHN BELL,
RORY COONEY, GARY DAIGLE, DARRYL DUCOTE, MARTY HAUGEN,
MICHAEL MAHLER, DONNA PEÑA, LEON ROBERTS, AND LORI TRUE

GIA Publications, Inc.
Chicago

G–6722

ISBN: 1-57999-545-4

GIA Publications, Inc.
7404 South Mason Avenue, Chicago, 60638
Copyright © 2005

CONTENTS

ACKNOWLEDGMENTS AND THANKS

Working on this resource has been a blessing and a wonderful challenge. I would first like to thank the folks at GIA Publications, especially Alec Harris for his tremendous friendship and forward-thinking vision in seeing the important link between liturgical music, prayer, and catechesis, and to Kelly Dobbs Mickus, Bob Batastini, Michael Cymbala, and Ed Harris for their support and longtime commitment to quality sung prayer. Thanks also to my good friend Diane Lampitt, as well as Cassie Nielsen, Sabrina Magnuson, Mary McCullough, and Jeffrey Burkholder at Harcourt Religion Publishers for their enthusiasm and passion for this approach of weaving liturgical prayer and music within the pedagogy of formation with youth. I want to commend and applaud the collaborative efforts of both GIA and Harcourt in providing such resources that celebrate and honor the rich connection between liturgy, music, prayer, catechesis, and youth ministry. The Church is truly blest because of this ministerial and publishing partnership.

Thanks are to be given to dear friends and fellow composers Tony Alonso, Michael Balhoff, John Bell, Rory Cooney, Gary Daigle, Darryl Ducote, Marty Haugen, Michael Joncas, Michael Mahler, Donna Peña, and Lori True for their wonderful compositions that enrich this project so beautifully and for the gift of their friendship. I also want to express additional thanks, love, and gratitude to Lori True and Fr. Jim Bessert, both of whom I have prepared and planned many liturgies and prayer services with over the years. I have learned much from their creativity, insights, and love of common prayer. And may God bless and keep Leon Roberts—how we miss him so.

I want to thank my former teacher, mentor, colleague, and good friend Art Zannoni for sharing and breaking open to me the many wonders of the scriptures over the years. I continue to learn much from him, and am thankful to God for his friendship and support in ministry.

Gratitude and love are to be shared with Rob and Mary Glover, Leisa Anslinger, Mary Werner, Bill Huebsch, Fr. Ray East, Joe Camacho, Sr. Kathleen Storms, SSND, Bonnie Faber, Sr. Gertrude Foley, SC, Jo Infante, Fr. George DeCosta, Sr. Roberta Kolasa, SJ, Sr. Andrea Lee, IHM, Barbara Conley-Waldmiller, and Dan Kantor for their tremendous loyalty, friendship, challenge, and inspiration in my life.

I also am delighted to express my appreciation and thanks to the faculty and staff at Benilde–St. Margaret's High School in St. Louis Park, Minnesota; to the people of St. Cecilia Parish in St. Paul for their authentic life of common prayer; and to the many team members and participants of "Music Ministry Alive!" who have been the source of tremendous joy and hope over the years. Thanks also to my parents and Helen for their tremendous love and support.

Finally, I want to thank the many young people and students whom I have had the pleasure, honor, and immense privilege to teach, to walk with, and to learn from. I dedicate these prayer celebrations to them in the spirit of their enthusiasm, outrageous hope and passion, and the lavish love and joy that I have received from each and every one of them over the years. God bless them all.

Soli Deo Gloria!

David Haas

INTRODUCTION

A Time to Pray: With the Old Testament is a collection of prayer celebrations for teenagers who are discovering the richness of the Hebrew scriptures in Catholic high schools, in parish youth ministries, and in catechetical and retreat programs. This volume is the beginning of an ongoing series of prayer services attempting to wed curricular content and liturgical prayer and music, centered in the belief that the faith stories of the scriptures, in order to be absorbed in the spirit of the message, must be celebrated prayerfully.

These services are designed and conceived in a way much different from many other resources of prayer for young people. The prayer celebrations found in these pages are based on the belief that young people are full members of the church NOW, and are presented using language and structure that treat them as adults. Secondly, they are intended to be experiences in which youth are invited to serve as leaders and as full participants, rather than "prayed at." Another unique aspect of these prayer celebrations is that they are shaped to serve gatherings where youths are either the primary participants, or at intergenerational events where young people pray with adults as well. No cute devices or gimmicks are used—only the strength of the Word that is proclaimed and prayed, the richness of symbols and repetitive ritual pattern, the power of the music chosen for reflection, and the faith-sharing elements that trust and reverence the wisdom that young people bring to prayer.

While these prayer celebrations were originally conceived to work in harmony with the newly revised senior high school textbook from Harcourt Religion Publishers, *Journey Through the Old Testament*, they can be adapted and used in partnership with other (curricular) texts and formational materials. In addition to their potential use in a "class" or "mini-course" program, these prayer services can also be used for a wide variety of settings and teen events: high school liturgical services or assemblies, youth retreats, parish youth group meetings, Confirmation preparation programs, and other prayer gatherings of young people. In short, these experiences were also intentionally designed to be adapted in parish and school settings where intergenerational events take place, especially for communities that have embraced "whole community catechesis" or the innovative *Generations of Faith* program. The accompanying CD (containing the music chosen for these prayer services) can also be used in a variety of settings where young people come together for prayer, or for inspirational listening.

PRINCIPLES IN USING THIS RESOURCE

The prayer celebrations found here follow a consistent format. Any ongoing gathering of communal prayer flourishes when a certain repetition and structure is in place ("knowable") by those who will pray together on a regular basis. While a variety of musical choices and scripture texts are suggested and available, the basic structure stays the same for each service.

Each of the prayer services can take place in a variety of environments: a classroom or other meeting room, a chapel or worship space, a multi-purpose facility, or a more relaxed, "homey" atmosphere. Each service should take no more than 15–20 minutes, and can be lengthened or shortened.

The first nine (9) prayer celebrations correspond to eight chapters and themes found in *Journey Through the Old Testament* (but are equally in harmony with many other high school Old Testament curricula available from other catechetical publishers). In a high school setting, they can take place any time during the study of the chapter (beginning, end, or any time throughout). In the parish or other youth ministry setting, they can be utilized for retreat experiences or other gatherings of prayer and formation. The remaining four (4) celebrations are seasonal in nature, one each for the seasons of Advent, Christmas, Lent, and Easter, and are designed for use for a variety of parish, retreat, and/or school settings. These four *seasonal* services are also celebrated through the "lens" of the Old Testament, and are especially adaptable not only for classroom settings or small groups, but for full school prayer assemblies or for parish and diocesan youth events as well.

It is important to understand that each of the prayer celebrations found in this resource are grounded in God's Word, particularly celebrated through the richness of the Old Testament, yet at the same time pointing toward our personal and communal *growth in Christ*. Another important aspect of these services is the opportunity for the participants to engage in faith sharing in the midst of common prayer, as is in line with the principles of whole community catechesis.

THE USE OF MUSIC

As with other prayer service compilations, music is an important and critical element in these prayer celebrations, but the implementation and use of music in these celebrations is presented in a way that is realistic. All of us who work with young people in both parish and school settings know and accept that the majority of young people (usually due to peer pressure and a heightened sense of self absorption) are not omfortable with participating in communal singing of [re]ligious or liturgical music. They tend not to sing in [pu]blic, especially not during liturgical celebrations of [an]y kind. This realization is the central consideration [as] to how music is to be utilized in these prayer [se]rvices. The music and the texts chosen are, however, [pr]imarily biblical and primarily *liturgical* and *communal* [in] nature.

While contemporary in terms of musical style in [m]ost cases, the music found here is purposely not [dr]awn from the presentation or theology found in [m]uch "Contemporary Christian Music" that is more [an]d more becoming a seductive influence on Catholic [yo]uth and young people of many other mainline and [lit]urgical Protestant communities. This music often [es]pouses an out-of-balance, "fundamentalist" biblical [st]ance, contributing to an overwhelming emphasis on [ou]r personal relationships with God and salvation, as [w]ell as an extreme emphasis on the performer him- or [he]rself. Even though it has already been stated and [re]cognized that many young people taking part in [th]ese services may not be drawn to sing, *liturgical* [m]usic still remains the center of our Catholic tradition, [an]d its participatory and more *communal* emphasis is [al]so a potentially powerful formational experience in [ca]techesis, as well as in liturgy, regardless of whether [yo]ung people actually "sing along." This is the kind of [m]usic at the center of this resource, and it emphasizes a [m]ore communal relationship with and *to* God and the [re]lationship of formation, catechesis, and the connection [to] the repertoire of Sunday worship (which is the time [an]d place where we are most authentically "Church").

With these principles and realities in mind, the [se]lections chosen for these prayer celebrations are [in]tended to be used *primarily* as recorded reflections [w]ith lyrics included within the celebration or at the [ba]ck of the book for participants to follow), although [pa]rticipants can also sing along if that wonderful [re]ality presents itself. In addition to the lyrics provided [an]d the accompanying CD, all of the musical selections [ar]e available in printed form, either in GIA's popular [hy]mnal *Gather Comprehensive—Second Edition*, in [se]parate sheet music, or in choral editions. In other [w]ords, the option for the students to sing is certainly [th]ere, but it is not required or essential for the prayer [ce]lebrations to be successful.

In addition to my own compositions, there are selec[ti]ons by well-known composers Tony Alonso, Michael [Ba]lhoff, John Bell, Rory Cooney, Gary Daigle, Darryl [D]ucote, Marty Haugen, Michael Mahler, Donna Peña, [Le]on Roberts, and Lori True that effectively echo and [am]plify the themes developed in *Journey Through the [O]ld Testament* and other high school and youth-oriented scripture programs. Many of these musical selections are well-known, tested treasures of contemporary repertoire, reflecting styles and genres that have proven to be appealing to young people. At the same time, these song-prayers provide solid content with a message that will help form and celebrate their spirituality and biblical faith, offering another resource for the catechist, teacher, youth minister, pastor, or other leader.

MINISTRIES AND ENVIRONMENT

The celebrations are most successful when the young people take part in ministry leadership roles. At a minimum, each service needs a *leader* (preferably this should be one of the young people, not the teacher, catechist, or visiting priest) and *two readers*. The young people taking part in these roles should be as well prepared as possible, and be encouraged to read and *pray* these texts carefully and slowly. The only symbols or materials (environment) needed are a candle, a Bible or lectionary placed in a prominent place, and a high-quality CD player.

Please note also that the pages for the prayer services can be reproduced at no charge by those who purchase this resource.

STRUCTURE FOR THE PRAYER CELEBRATIONS

As stated earlier, each of the prayer celebrations has stable and consistent elements and other moments that vary. The structural flow for each service is as follows:

Opening Invitation to Prayer

Here, the leader sets the tone for the entire celebration.

Opening Song/Refrain

The common refrain "God Is Here" is used for each of the services. After a while, the young people (and other participants) hopefully will actually feel more comfortable in singing along with this short, repeated refrain, which is sung several times like a centering mantra.

Dialogue to Welcome the Word

This dialogue between the leader and participants prepares all to truly hear, listen, and reflect on the Word of God.

Reading(s) from the Word of God

This is a dialogical and participatory proclamation of a particular scripture reading or several scriptural passages woven together in harmony with the focus of the chapter theme and intent of the time of prayer. These are paraphrases—poetic and creative conversational renderings that attempt to involve the participants along with the two readers. This participatory design will hopefully engage the young people more intimately with the texts.

Song of Reflection

Then, a musical reflection is played from the accompanying CD, a song or selection that amplifies the theme/focus of the chapter and/or celebration. As many as three options are given for each celebration.

Reflection Questions

In line with the spirit of "whole community catechesis," two pointed questions are provided as staring points for reflection and discussion based on the scripture readings and musical selections. An option for concluding this time of sharing would be for the participants to sing or listen to the refrain of "Take, O Take Me As I Am."

Intercessions

Intercessory prayer is an important element of any time of communal prayer, and four are provided for each celebration, tailored to the particular focus, also providing an opportunity for the participants to offer their own prayers.

The Lord's Prayer

The Lord's Prayer begins the conclusion of the celebration, and a distinct introduction is provided for each service.

Final Blessing

The final blessing concludes the service, and it can be recited or sung using the text of Lori True's "May the Road Rise to Meet You."

Sign of Peace

All share the sign of peace. The prayer can conclude here, or another song (suggested from the list for each prayer service) can be used to conclude.

A FINAL WORD

These guidelines are just that—guidelines. Feel free adapt these services to your particular setting and si ation. The most important aspect is that a certain se of repetition and ritual memory be established, that young people participate as fully as possible, and t the leaders and readers are well prepared. Stay in tou with us and let us know how these celebrations working in your school and parish settings.

It is my hope, and that of GIA Publications a Harcourt Religion Publishers, that these prayer ce brations can become a prayerful, musical, and grow filled foundation for your ministry with the you people of God.

God bless you!

David Haas
Eagan, Minnesota

A TIME TO PRAY:
WITH THE OLD TESTAMENT

COMPACT DISC INFORMATION

Music by David Haas

with Tony Alonso, Michael Balhoff, John Bell, Rory Cooney, Gary Daigle, Darryl Ducote, Marty Haugen, Michael Mahler, Donna Peña, Leon Roberts, and Lori True.

Provided after each song listed is the reference for where the particular selection can be found in *Gather Comprehensive—Second Edition* (GC2), available as a separate printed edition, or both.

CD 1

COMMON MUSICAL RESPONSES
1 – God Is Here – David Haas (G-6687)
2 – Take, O Take Me As I Am – John Bell (GC2# 692, G-5285)
3 – May the Road Rise to Meet You – Lori True (G-6066)

GOD AND HIS CHOSEN PEOPLE
4 – Deep Within – David Haas (GC2 #419, G-3338)
5 – I Lift My Soul – Lori True (GC2 #562, G-6556)

THE CREATION OF GOD'S PEOPLE
6 – We Praise You – Gary Daigle, Darryl Ducote, Michael Balhoff (GC2 #540, G-5399)
7 – You Are the Presence – David Haas (G-3506)
8 – The Hand of God – David Haas (GC2 #828, G-5663)

GOD'S PEOPLE AND THE PROMISED LAND
9 – Who Is the Alien – Lori True/Mary Louise Bringle (G-6711)
10 – You Will Find Me in Your Heart – David Haas (G-4347)
11 – Everlasting Grace Is Yours – David Haas (G-4346)

BUILDING THE KINGDOM
12 – We Praise You – David Haas (GC2 #521, G-5814)
13 – Oh, Lordy-O! – Donna Peña (G-4061)
14 – Lord, It Is Good – David Haas (G-4800)

THE KINGDOM DIVIDED AND THE EXILE
15 – We Are Called – David Haas (GC2 #710, G-3292)
16 – Share Your Bread with the Hungry – David Haas (G-4734)
17 – Show Me the Path – David Haas (G-3927)

THE RESTORATION AND NEW BEGINNINGS
18 – You Are Mine – David Haas (GC2 #627, G-3656)
19 – I Am for You – Rory Cooney (GC2 #676, G-3967)
20 – Turn My Heart, O God – Marty Haugen (GC2 #561, G-5864)

CD 2

A FUTURE BUILT ON PROMISE
1 – With You By My Side – David Haas (GC2 #623, G-5008)
2 – We Choose Life – David Haas (G-4687)
3 – Shepherd Me, O God – Marty Haugen (GC2 #23, G-2950)

THE WISDOM OF ISRAEL
4 – Let Us Sing – Lori True (G-6401)
5 – I Thirst for You – David Haas (G-4688)
6 – They Who Do Justice – David Haas (GC2 #17, G-3333)
7 – Like Burning Incense, O Lord – Lori True (G-6401)
8 – Let Us Go Rejoicing – Leon Roberts (G-4606)
9 – Here I Am – Tony Alonso (G-6401)

CELEBRATING ADVENT
10 – Warm the Time of Winter – Lori True/Ruth Duck (GC2 #339, G-5209)
11 – Make Us Worthy – Michael Mahler (GC2 #557, G-6043)

CELEBRATING CHRISTMAS

12 – *Great Joy* – David Haas (G-5201)

13 – *The Encounter* – David Haas/Jaroslav Vajda (G-5219)

14 – *Carol of the Child* – David Haas (G-4344)

CELEBRATING LENT

15 – *Return to the Lord* – David Haas (GC2 #415, G-6160)

16 – *I Am Standing Waiting* – Tony Alonso/Shirley Erena Murray (G-5612)

17 – *The Harvest of Justice* – David Haas (GC2 #716, G-3582)

CELEBRATING EASTER

18 – *Come and See* – Michael Mahler (G-6041)

19 – *Alleluia! Let Us Rejoice* – David Haas (G-3079)

20 – *God Has Done Marvelous Things* – David Haas/Herbert Brokering (G-4731)

PRAYER CELEBRATIONS

WILL PLANT MY LAW
A CELEBRATION OF GOD'S WORD IN OUR LIVES

Environment: *In place should be a Bible, attractive in appearance, open and displayed on a table with a candle next to it.*

OPENING

As the leader begins to speak, someone from the group comes forward to light the candle.

Leader   As we begin this time of prayer,
we gather around the light of the Lord
to enlighten us,
to guide us, to challenge us.
May this light help all of us
to remember and celebrate that God is here.

Listen or sing along as the song is played.

God Is Here
(CD 1, Track 1)

God is here, God is here.
One thing I know – God is here.
God is here, God is here.
One thing I know – God is here.

Words and music by David Haas.
Copyright © 2004 GIA Publications, Inc.
Used with permission. All rights reserved.

INVITATION TO HEAR THE WORD OF GOD

Leader   Gracious and awesome God,
we know that you are here.
Open our minds to listen well
and hear the wisdom you bring!

All   Gracious and awesome God,
we know that you are here.
Open our lips to speak boldly
and proclaim your truth in love!

Leader   Gracious and awesome God,
we know that you are here.
Open our hearts
to generously receive the gift of your Word!

All   Gracious and awesome God,
we know that you are here.
Do not be silent!
Speak to us!

Leader   Let us now hear and listen well
to these passages from the Word of God.

THE WORD OF GOD

> Isaiah 1:10; 2:3
> Jeremiah 1:4–10, 31
> *Adapted by David Haas*

Reader 1 These words are adapted from the prophets Isaiah and Jeremiah.

Reader 2 Hear the Word of God, all of you!

Reader 1 Listen to the *teaching* of our God!

All Hear the Word of the Lord!

Reader 2 Come, let us go up to the mountain of God!

Reader 1 Come, let us go to the house of Jacob!

Reader 2 The Word of God came to me, saying: "Before I formed you in your mother's womb, *I knew you.*"

All Hear the Word of the Lord!

Reader 1 "Before you were born, *I honored you.*"

Reader 2 "I have appointed you to be *prophets* to the nations."

All Hear the Word of the Lord!

Reader 1 But then I cried out to God: "I do not know how to speak!"

Reader 2 "I am young."

All I am young!

Reader 1 But the Word spoke *again*, saying to me:

Reader 2 "Do not say, 'I am young'; for you shall go to those to whom I *send you.*"

Reader 1 "You shall speak the words *I choose.*"

Reader 2 "Do not be afraid."

All May we not be afraid!

Reader 1 "I am *with* you, and I will deliver you.

Reader 2 "I have put my words into your mout See, on this very day, I call you to *go out.*"

Reader 1 "I call you to go out everywhere, to *pluck up and pull down.*"

Reader 2 "I call you to *destroy* and to *overthrow.*"

Reader 1 "I call you to *build* and to *plant.*"

Reader 2 "Listen, now, this generation: behold, *hear* the Word of God."

All Hear the Word of God!

Reader 2 These words are from God and the servants of God.

All We give thanks to God for the gift of this Word. May we follow Christ and deepen our call to faith.

Pause for silent reflection.

SONG OF REFLECTION

Leader At this time let us listen to a song of reflection, which recalls God's presence in our lives.

Song is chosen from one of the following:

– Deep Within *(CD 1, Track 4)*
– I Lift My Soul *(CD 1, Track 5)*

QUESTIONS FOR REFLECTION & FAITH SHARING

• *What is the best way for us to truly hear God's Word?*

• *How can we pray these words and discover God's plan for us?*

• *What things in our lives, our relationships, and in the world are we to "pluck up," "pull down," "destroy and overthrow," or "build and plant"?*

Listen or sing/pray along as the song is played. ——————

Take, O Take Me As I Am
(CD 1, Track 2)

Take, O take me as I am;
summon out what I shall be;
set your seal upon my heart
and live in me.

Words and music by John Bell Copyright © 1995 Iona Community/ GIA Publications, Inc. Used with permission. All rights reserved.

INTERCESSIONS

Leader   Let us now place our prayers before God.

We pray for us all, God's chosen people;
called to seek God in all things
and to serve each other.

We pray:

All   Lord, hear our prayer.

Leader   We pray for all who lead:
all those who make decisions for our world
and for our future.

We pray:

All   Lord, hear our prayer.

Leader   We pray for those
who continually seek God's voice of hope in their lives:
the poor, the hungry, the suffering, the afraid, and all
who long for happiness.

We pray:

All   Lord, hear our prayer.

Leader   We pray for those who are close to us,
and for all who may be suffering in any way.

We pray:

Participants can name those for whom they want to pray.

All   Lord, hear our prayer.

Leader   We pray for any other needs
that we may have at this time.

Participants offer any prayers that they may have. At the conclusion of their prayers, the leader continues.

For all of these prayers and for those
that lie deep within our hearts.

We pray:

All   Lord, hear our prayer.

THE LORD'S PRAYER

Leader   Gracious and awesome God,
we know that you are with us here.
We believe that you have called
each and every one of us
to hear and listen to your voice,
to follow the guidance of your Word.

We are ready to live by this Word,
for we believe it is your voice,
and we know that we belong to you.

So we offer and surrender ourselves
to your guidance in our lives
as we pray:

All   Our Father,
who art in heaven,
hallowed be thy name;
thy kingdom come;
thy will be done on earth
as it is in heaven.
Give us this day our daily bread;
and forgive us our trespasses
as we forgive those
who trespass against us;
and lead us not into temptation,
but deliver us from evil.
For the kingdom,
the power and the glory are yours,
now and forever. Amen.

FINAL BLESSING/SIGN OF PEACE

Leader   Let us now all bless one another.

All raise their hands in blessing of one another.

Sing or recite the words to this blessing.

Leader   Let us now end this time of prayer
by sharing with each other
a sign of peace and friendship in Christ.

May the Road Rise to Meet
You *(CD 1, Track 3)*

May the road rise to meet you.
May the wind be at your back.
May the sun shine warm upon
  your face, upon your face.
May the rain fall softly on
  your fields,
And until we meet again,
may you keep safe in the
gentle, loving arms of God.

*Words and music by Lori True.
Copyright © 2003 GIA Publications, Inc.
Used with permission. All rights reserved.*

*A*ll Your Works Are Wonderful
A Celebration Remembering the Wonders of God

Opening
As the leader begins to speak, someone from the group comes forward to light the candle.

Leader   As we begin this time of prayer,
we gather around the light of the Lord
to enlighten us,
to guide us, to challenge us.
May this light help all of us
to remember and celebrate that God is here.

Listen or sing along as the song is played. ————

Invitation to Hear the Word of God

Leader   Gracious and awesome God,
we know that you are here.
Open our minds to listen well
and hear the wisdom you bring!

All   Gracious and awesome God,
we know that you are here.
Open our lips to speak boldly
and proclaim your truth in love!

Leader   Gracious and awesome God,
we know that you are here.
Open our hearts
to generously receive the gift of your Word!

All   Gracious and awesome God,
we know that you are here.
Do not be silent!
Speak to us!

Leader   Let us now hear and listen well
to these passages from the Word of God.

Environment: In place should be a Bible, attractive in appearance, open and displayed on a table with a candle next to it.

God Is Here
(CD 1, Track 1)

God is here, God is here.
One thing I know – God is here.
God is here, God is here.
One thing I know – God is here.

Words and music by David Haas.
Copyright © 2004 GIA Publications, Inc.
Used with permission. All rights reserved.

THE WORD OF GOD

> 1 Chronicles 16: 8–17
> Psalm 105: 1–6
> Psalm 106: 7–12, 19–21
> Psalm 107: 8–9, 31–32
> Psalm 139: 14
> *Adapted by Daivd Haas*

Reader 1   These words are adapted from 1 Chronicles and from the Book of Psalms.

Reader 2   Give thanks to God! Praise God's name!

Reader 1   Make the wonderful deeds of God known to everyone!

All   God, all your works are wonderful!

Reader 2   Let all who seek to have God in their lives – let them rejoice!

Reader 1   *Remember* the wonderful works God has done, *all* of the miracles, *all* of God's decisions and judgments!

Reader 2   *Remember* that God has chosen *each and every one of us*!

All   God, all your works are wonderful!

Reader 1   *Remember* and celebrate God's promise to us, God's most holy Word, the Word that began *so long ago* and still speaks to us *now.*

Reader 2   These promises were kept to Abraham, to Issac;

Reader 1   To Jacob, to all of Israel, and to *all of us*!

All   God, all your works are wonderful!

Reader 2   Tell everyone you can about the wonderful works of God!

Reader 1   *Remember* how God did not abandon those in slavery in Egypt.

Reader 2   *Remember* that while they forgot and abandoned their relationship with God, God did *not* forget them.

Reader 1   God saved them, and he made the Red Sea into dry land, leading them to *safety.*

All   God, all your works are wonderful!

Reader 2   *Remember* how God did *not* destroy them when they worshipped a false God, when they forgot the great things done for them.

Reader 1   Rather, God *remained faithful*, God *remained their God.*

Reader 2   For God is "love unending"! God *satisfies* the thirsty, and the hungry are *filled* with good things.

Reader 1   Let us not forget to thank God always and *remember God's unconditional love.*

Reader 2   Let everyone sing and offer praise, whenever we gather together in God's name.

All   God, all your works are wonderful!

Reader 1   We praise you, for we are *wonderfully* made!

All   We praise you, for we are *wonderfully* made! God, all your works are wonderful!

Reader 2   These words are from God and the servants of God.

All   We give thanks to God for the gift of this Word. May we follow Christ an deepen our call to faith.

Pause for silent reflection.

SONG OF REFLECTION

Leader   At this time let us listen to a song of reflection, challenging us all to listen to the call of Christ to follow him in faith.

Song is chosen from one of the following:

– We Praise You *(CD 1, Track 6)*
– You Are the Presence *(CD 1, Track 7)*
– The Hand of God *(CD 1, Track 8)*

QUESTIONS FOR REFLECTION & FAITH SHARING

- *What are the "wonderful works of God" that we easily forget and need to always hold close to our memories and hearts?*

- *What are those things (or who are those people) that are living and vibrant signs of God's wonderful activity in our lives?*

Listen or sing/pray along as the song is played.

INTERCESSIONS

Take, O Take Me As I Am
(CD 1, Track 2)

Take, O take me as I am;
summon out what I shall be;
set your seal upon my heart
and live in me.

Leader   Let us now place our prayers before God.

We pray for us all, God's wonderful works of art,
called to remember God's action in our lives,
and to respond in service to each other.

We pray:

All   Lord, hear our prayer.

Leader   We pray for all who lead:
all those who make decisions for our world
and for our future.

We pray:

All   Lord, hear our prayer.

Leader   We pray for those
who continually seek to find signs of
God's beauty in the world, in the midst
of hunger, poverty, and suffering.

We pray:

All   Lord, hear our prayer.

Leader   We pray for those close to us,
and for all who may be suffering in any way.

We pray:

All   Lord, hear our prayer.

Participants can name those for whom they want to pray.

Leader   We pray for any other needs
that we may have at this time.

For all of these prayers and for those
that lie deep within our hearts.

We pray:

All   Lord, hear our prayer.

Participants offer any prayers that they may have. At the conclusion of their prayers, the leader continues.

THE LORD'S PRAYER

Leader   Gracious and awesome God,
we know that you are with us here,
and we see your presence
in the wonderful things around us.
We believe that you have called
each and every one of us
to hear and listen to your voice,
and to respond by giving you
thanks for all that you have done for us.

These are the living signs and reminders
that we belong to you.

So we offer and surrender ourselves
to your guidance in our lives
as we pray:

All   Our Father,
who art in heaven,
hallowed be thy name;
thy kingdom come;
thy will be done on earth
as it is in heaven.
Give us this day our daily bread;
and forgive us our trespasses
as we forgive those
who trespass against us;
and lead us not into temptation,
but deliver us from evil.
For the kingdom,
the power and the glory are yours,
now and forever. Amen.

FINAL BLESSING/SIGN OF PEACE

Leader   Let us now all bless one another.

All raise their hands in blessing of one another.

Sing or recite the words to this blessing.

Leader   Let us now end this time of prayer
by sharing with each other
a sign of peace and friendship in Christ.

May the Road Rise to Meet
You *(CD 1, Track 3)*
May the road rise to meet you.
May the wind be at your back.
May the sun shine warm upon
  your face, upon your face.
May the rain fall softly on
  your fields,
And until we meet again,
may you keep safe in the
gentle, loving arms of God.

Who Is The Alien?
A Celebration of God's Open Heart to All

OPENING

As the leader begins to speak, someone from the group comes forward to light the candle.

Leader   As we begin this time of prayer,
we gather around the light of the Lord
to enlighten us,
to guide us, to challenge us.
May this light help all of us
to remember and celebrate that God is here.

Listen or sing along as the song is played. ————

INVITATION TO HEAR THE WORD OF GOD

Leader   Gracious and awesome God,
we know that you are here.
Open our minds to listen well
and hear the wisdom you bring!

All   Gracious and awesome God,
we know that you are here.
Open our lips to speak boldly
and proclaim your truth in love!

Leader   Gracious and awesome God,
we know that you are here.
Open our hearts
to generously receive the gift of your Word!

All   Gracious and awesome God,
we know that you are here.
Do not be silent!
Speak to us!

Leader   Let us now hear and listen well
to these passages from the Word of God.

Environment: In place should be a Bible, attractive in appearance, open and displayed on a table with a candle next to it.

God Is Here
(CD 1, Track 1)

God is here, God is here.
One thing I know – God is here.
God is here, God is here.
One thing I know – God is here.

Words and music by David Haas.
Copyright © 2004 GIA Publications, Inc.
Used with permission. All rights reserved.

The Word of God

> Exodus 3:7
> Leviticus 19:3–34
> Deuteronomy 24:17
> Jeremiah 29:11
> *Adapted by David Haas*

Reader 1 These words come to us from the Book of Exodus.

Reader 2 God said:
"I have seen the misery of my people;
I have heard their cry –
indeed, *I know their sufferings*."

Reader 1 "I have come to deliver them,
to bring them to a land
flowing with milk and honey."

Reader 2 And these words of challenge come to us from Leviticus and Deuteronomy.

Reader 1 When those who are seen as *aliens*
come to stay with you,
you shall not oppress them.

Reader 2 We should not deprive anything from those who are *orphans of justice*.

Reader 1 They shall be seen as we see each other – as citizens, one with us.

All We should love the alien *as we love ourselves*.

Reader 2 For remember,
you too once were aliens
in the land of Egypt.

Reader 1 And these words of comfort come to us from the prophet Jeremiah.

Reader 2 God says to us:
I know the plans I have for you,
plans for your *well being, not for harm*.

Reader 1 My plans are for all of you
to have a future *filled with hope*.

All A future with *hope*.

Reader 2 When you call upon me,
when you *pray to me*,
know that I will hear you.

Reader 1 If you *search* for me, *you will find me*.

Reader 2 If you seek me with *all* of your heart –

Reader 1 I will let you *find* me.

Reader 2 I will restore all your treasures
and *gather you together again*.

Reader 1 I will *bring you* back.

Reader 2 I will *bring you* back.

All I will *bring you back*.

Reader 1 These words are from God and the servants of God.

All We give thanks to God for the gift of this Word. May we follow Christ and deepen our call to faith.

Pause for silent reflection.

Song of Reflection

Leader At this time let us listen to a song of reflection.

Song is chosen from one of the following:

– Who Is the Alien? *(CD 1, Track 9)*
– You Will Find Me in Your Heart *(CD 1, Track 10)*
– Everlasting Grace Is Yours *(CD 1, Track 11)*

QUESTIONS FOR REFLECTION & FAITH SHARING

- **Who are the aliens in our world and church today? How can we intentionally reach out to them?**

- **When have we felt like an "alien" on the "outside" of the circle or community of the favored?**

Listen or sing/pray along as the song is played.

INTERCESSIONS

Take, O Take Me As I Am
(CD 1, Track 2)

Take, O take me as I am;
summon out what I shall
be; set your seal upon my
heart and live in me.

Words and music by John Bell.
Copyright © 1995 Iona Community/
GIA Publications, Inc. Used with
permission. All rights reserved.

Leader	Let us now place our prayers before God.
	We pray for us all, God's family, called to remember God's love and acceptance, and to respond with care to each other.
	We pray:
All	Lord, hear our prayer.
Leader	We pray for all who lead: all those who make decisions for our world and for our future.
	We pray:
All	Lord, hear our prayer.
Leader	We pray for those who continually see themselves as aliens and outsiders, all those who suffer and seek to be one with the human family.
	We pray:
All	Lord, hear our prayer.
Leader	We pray for those who are close to us, and for all who may be suffering in any way.
	We pray:
All	Lord, hear our prayer.
Leader	We pray for any other needs that we may have at this time.
	For all of these prayers and for those that lie deep within our hearts.
	We pray:
All	Lord, hear our prayer.

Participants can name those for whom they want to pray.

Participants offer any prayers that they may have. At the conclusion of their prayers, the leader continues.

THE LORD'S PRAYER

Leader   Gracious and awesome God,
we know that you are with us here,
and we see your presence
in the wonderful things around us.
We believe that you have called
each and every one of us
to be close to you, to be one with you.

So we offer and surrender ourselves
to your guidance in our lives
as we pray:

All   Our Father,
who art in heaven,
hallowed be thy name;
thy kingdom come;
thy will be done on earth
as it is in heaven.
Give us this day our daily bread;
and forgive us our trespasses
as we forgive those
who trespass against us;
and lead us not into temptation,
but deliver us from evil.
For the kingdom,
the power and the glory are yours,
now and forever. Amen.

FINAL BLESSING/SIGN OF PEACE

Leader   Let us now all bless one another.

All raise their hands in blessing of one another.

Sing or recite the words to this blessing.

Leader   Let us now end this time of prayer
by sharing with each other
a sign of peace and friendship in Christ.

May the Road Rise to Meet You *(CD 1, Track 3)*

May the road rise to meet you.
May the wind be at your back.
May the sun shine warm upon
  your face, upon your face.
May the rain fall softly on
  your fields,
And until we meet again,
may you keep safe in the
gentle, loving arms of God.

Words and music by Lori True.
Copyright © 2003 GIA Publications, Inc.
Used with permission. All rights reserved.

You Are Always Near

A Celebration of Praise and Thanks to Our Faithful God

Opening

*As the leader begins to speak, someone from the group
comes forward to light the candle.*

Leader   As we begin this time of prayer,
we gather around the light of the Lord
to enlighten us,
to guide us, to challenge us.
May this light help all of us
to remember and celebrate that God is here.

Listen or sing along as the song is played. ——————

Invitation to Hear the Word of God

Leader   Gracious and awesome God,
we know that you are here.
Open our minds to listen well
and hear the wisdom you bring!

All   Gracious and awesome God,
we know that you are here.
Open our lips to speak boldly
and proclaim your truth in love!

Leader   Gracious and awesome God,
we know that you are here.
Open our hearts
to generously receive the gift of your Word!

All   Gracious and awesome God,
we know that you are here.
Do not be silent!
Speak to us!

Leader   Let us now hear and listen well
to these passages from the Word of God.

*Environment: In place should be a Bible,
attractive in appearance, open and
displayed on a table with a candle next to it.*

God Is Here
(CD 1, Track 1)

God is here, God is here.
One thing I know – God is here.
God is here, God is here.
One thing I know – God is here.

*Words and music by David Haas.
Copyright © 2004 GIA Publications, Inc.
Used with permission. All rights reserved.*

THE WORD OF GOD

2 Samuel 22:4–7, 20, 31–34, 37
Nehemiah 9:5b
Adapted by David Haas.

Reader 1 These words are adapted from the books of Second Samuel and Nehemiah.

Reader 2 I call upon the name of God!

Reader 1 Our God, who is *worthy* to be praised!

All God is *worthy* to be praised!

Reader 2 God has saved us from our enemies!

Reader 1 In my distress I called upon God;
I called out to God
and *my voice was heard.*

Reader 2 God brought me out from my fear,
to a safe place.
God *delivered* me,
God *delighted* in me.

All God is worthy to be praised!

Reader 1 This God is *perfect.*

Reader 2 The promise of God is to be believed,
for God is a shield
for all who seek help.

Reader 1 Who else is God – *except for God?*
Who else is our rock – *except for God?*

Reader 2 God has given me strength,
and opened wide my path.

Reader 1 God has made my feet like those of
the deer, and set me *safe and secure.*

All God is worthy to be praised!

Reader 2 God *lives!* Blessed be my rock!

Reader 1 May God be praised!

Reader 2 Everyone –
praise the Lord everywhere!
Sing and shout praise to God!

Reader 1 God is a *tower* of salvation, showing
unconditional love for all who lead.

Reader 2 Stand up! *Bless* the Lord!

All Stand up! *Bless* the Lord!

Reader 1 Stand up and bless the Lord
for ever and ever!

All God is worthy to be praised!

Reader 2 These words are from God and the
servants of God.

All We give thanks to God
for the gift of this Word.
May we follow Christ
and deepen our call to faith.

Pause for silent reflection.

SONG OF REFLECTION

Leader At this time let us listen to a song of
reflection, which challenges us all to
take up our cross and walk the walk
of self giving.

Song is chosen from one of the following:

– We Praise You *(CD 1, Track 12)*
– Oh, Lordy-O! *(CD 1, Track 13)*
– Lord, It Is Good *(CD 1, Track 14)*

QUESTIONS FOR REFLECTION & FAITH SHARING

• Why are praise and thanksgiving so important to us as people of faith?

• In a world filled with so much suffering, pain, and sadness, how can we continue to praise God?

Listen or sing/pray along as the song is played. —————

Take, O Take Me As I Am
(CD 1, Track 2)

Take, O take me as I am;
summon out what I shall be;
set your seal upon my heart
and live in me.

*Words and music by John Bell.
Copyright © 1995 Iona Community/
GIA Publications, Inc. Used with
permission. All rights reserved.*

INTERCESSIONS

Leader Let us now place our prayers before God.

We pray for us all, God's people,
called to give thanks in all things
as we strive to make a better world.

We pray:

All Lord, hear our prayer.

Leader We pray for all who lead: all those who make decisions
for our world and for our future.

We pray:

All Lord, hear our prayer.

Leader We pray for those
who praise God even in the midst
of fear, anxiety, and distress.

We pray:

All Lord, hear our prayer.

Leader We pray for those who are close to us,
and for all who may be suffering in any way.

*Participants can name those
for whom they want to pray.*

We pray:

All Lord, hear our prayer.

Leader We pray for any other needs
that we may have at this time.

*Participants offer any prayers
that they may have. At the
conclusion of their prayers,
the leader continues.*

For all of these prayers and for those that lie deep
within our hearts.

We pray:

All Lord, hear our prayer.

THE LORD'S PRAYER

Leader   Gracious and awesome God,
we praise and thank you
for so many wonderful things.
We believe that you have called
each and every one of us
to be attentive
to the wonders around us.
We come before you,
offering our thanks for all that you have done for us.

So we offer and surrender ourselves
to your guidance in our lives
as we pray:

All   Our Father,
who art in heaven,
hallowed be thy name;
thy kingdom come;
thy will be done on earth
as it is in heaven.
Give us this day our daily bread;
and forgive us our trespasses
as we forgive those
who trespass against us;
and lead us not into temptation,
but deliver us from evil.
For the kingdom,
the power and the glory are yours,
now and forever. Amen.

May the Road Rise to Meet You *(CD 1, Track 3)*

May the road rise to meet you.
May the wind be at your back.
May the sun shine warm upon
   your face, upon your face.
May the rain fall softly on
   your fields,
And until we meet again,
may you keep safe in the
gentle, loving arms of God.

Words and music by Lori True.
Copyright © 2003 GIA Publications, Inc.
Used with permission. All rights reserved.

FINAL BLESSING/SIGN OF PEACE

Leader   Let us now all bless one another.

All raise their hands in blessing of one another.

Sing or recite the words to this blessing.

Leader   Let us now end this time of prayer
by sharing with each other
a sign of peace and friendship in Christ.

Walk HUMBLY WITH GOD

A CELEBRATION OF OUR CALL TO SEEK JUSTICE

OPENING

As the leader begins to speak, someone from the group comes forward to light the candle.

Leader
As we begin this time of prayer,
we call forth the light of Christ
to enlighten us, to guide us, to challenge us.
May this light help all of us
to remember and celebrate that God is here.

Listen or sing along as the song is played.

INVITATION TO HEAR THE WORD OF GOD

Leader
Gracious and awesome God,
we know that you are here.
Open our minds to listen well
and hear the wisdom you bring!

All
Gracious and awesome God,
we know that you are here.
Open our lips to speak boldly
and proclaim your truth in love!

Leader
Gracious and awesome God,
we know that you are here.
Open our hearts
to generously receive the gift of your Word!

All
Gracious and awesome God,
we know that you are here.
Do not be silent!
Speak to us!

Leader
Let us now hear and listen well,
to these passages from the Word of God.

Environment: In place should be a Bible, attractive in appearance, open and displayed on a table with a candle next to it.

God Is Here
(CD 1, Track 1)

God is here, God is here.
One thing I know – God is here.
God is here, God is here.
One thing I know – God is here.

*Words and music by David Haas.
Copyright © 2004 GIA Publications, Inc.
Used with permission. All rights reserved.*

THE WORD OF GOD

Isaiah 58: 3–4, 6–12
Micah 6:8
Adapted by David Haas

Reader 1   These words are taken from the prophets Isaiah and Micah.

Reader 2   The people asked God:
"Why do we fast?
Why should we *humble* ourselves,
if you do not notice?"

Reader 1   God speaks:"You fast and serve your *own interests,* and you oppress all who are in your care."

All   Walk humbly with God.

Reader 2   "You fast only to argue, fight, and strike with a wicked fist."

Reader 1   "Such fasting will *never* be heard or seen by God."

Reader 2   "This is the fast that *I* choose:
to *loose* the bonds of *injustice,*
to *break* every yoke,
and let the *oppressed go free.*"

All   Walk humbly with God.

Reader 1   "*Share* your bread with the hungry."

Reader 2   "*Welcome the poor* to your home."

Reader 1   "Then your light shall break forth like the dawn."

Reader 2   "Your *healing* shall spring up quickly."

Reader 1   "Your *dignity* shall go forth before you, and the *glory* of God shall keep you safe. You shall call, and God *will* answer, you shall cry, and God will be there."

Reader 2   "If you remove all oppression from your midst, and the shame of those who may harm you, if you offer you bread to the hungry,
your light shall rise in the darkness."

All   Walk humbly with God.

Reader 1   "God will always guide you, satisfy your needs in places of thirst, and make your bones *strong.*"

Reader 2   "You will be like a watered garden, like a spring whose waters *never fail.*"

Reader 1   "Your ancient buildings, old and brok down, will be rebuilt."

All   We will be called the *"repairers of th breach,"* the *"restorers of broken households."*

Reader 2   *Remember* what God has required o us:

All   Do justice,
love kindness,
and walk *humbly* with God.

Reader 1   These words are from God and the servants of God.

All   We give thanks to God for the gift of this Word. May we follow Christ and deepen our call to faith.

Pause for silent reflection.

SONG OF REFLECTION

Leader   At this time let us listen to this song reflection, and allow the healing pow of Christ to come and enter our hear and minds.

Song is chosen from one of the following:

– We Are Called *(CD 1, Track 15)*
– Share Your Bread With the Hungry *(CD 1, Track 16*
– Show Me the Path *(CD 1, Track 17)*

QUESTIONS FOR REFLECTION & FAITH SHARING

• *What does it mean for me, or for any of us, to live as the "repairer of the breach"?*

• *Where does injustice still reside in our world, and what should our response be as God's people?*

Listen or sing/pray along as the song is played. ───────

INTERCESSIONS

Leader	Let us now place our prayers before God.
	We pray for us all, the Body of Christ: called to be in relationship with Christ and to be vessels of healing in the world.
	We pray:
All	Lord, hear our prayer.
Leader	We pray for all who lead: all those who make decisions for our world and for our future.
	We pray:
All	Lord, hear our prayer.
Leader	We pray for those who suffer injustices of every kind: discrimination and hatred, hunger and homelessness, abuse and abandonment, victims of war and torture and so many other wrongs.
	We pray:
All	Lord, hear our prayer.
Leader	We pray for those who are close to us, and for all who may be suffering in any way.
	We pray:
All	Lord, hear our prayer.
Leader	We pray for any other needs that we may have at this time.
	For all of these prayers and for those that lie deep within our hearts.
	We pray:
All	Lord, hear our prayer.

Participants can name those for whom they want to pray.

Participants offer any prayers that they may have. At the conclusion of their prayers, the leader continues.

THE LORD'S PRAYER

Leader   Gracious and awesome God,
we know that you are with us here,
and we see your presence
in the many blessings that we have received.
We believe that you have called
each and every one of us
to act in your name,
to become agents of justice,
to truly be "the repairers of the breach."

So we offer and surrender ourselves
to your guidance in our lives
as we pray:

All   Our Father,
who art in heaven,
hallowed be thy name;
thy kingdom come;
thy will be done on earth
as it is in heaven.
Give us this day our daily bread;
and forgive us our trespasses
as we forgive those
who trespass against us;
and lead us not into temptation,
but deliver us from evil.
For the kingdom,
the power and the glory are yours,
now and forever. Amen.

May the Road Rise to Meet You *(CD 1, Track 3)*

May the road rise to meet you.
May the wind be at your back.
May the sun shine warm upon
   your face, upon your face.
May the rain fall softly on
   your fields,
And until we meet again,
may you keep safe in the
gentle, loving arms of God.

FINAL BLESSING/SIGN OF PEACE

Leader   Let us now all bless one another.

All raise their hands in blessing of one another.

Sing or recite the words to this blessing.

Leader   Let us now end this time of prayer
by sharing with each other
a sign of peace and friendship in Christ.

WILL BRING YOU HOME

A CELEBRATION OF HEALING AND CONVERSION

OPENING

As the leader begins to speak, someone from the group comes forward to light the candle.

Leader
As we begin this time of prayer,
we gather around the light of the Lord
to enlighten us,
to guide us, to challenge us.
May this light help all of us
to remember and celebrate that God is here.

Listen or sing along as the song is played.

INVITATION TO HEAR THE WORD OF GOD

Leader
Gracious and awesome God,
we know that you are here.
Open our minds to listen well
and hear the wisdom you bring!

All
Gracious and awesome God,
we know that you are here.
Open our lips to speak boldly
and proclaim your truth in love!

Leader
Gracious and awesome God,
we know that you are here.
Open our hearts
to generously receive the gift of your Word!

All
Gracious and awesome God,
we know that you are here.
Do not be silent!
Speak to us!

Leader
Let us now hear and listen well
to these passages from the Word of God.

Environment: In place should be a Bible, attractive in appearance, open and displayed on a table with a candle next to it.

God Is Here
(CD 1, Track 1)

God is here, God is here.
One thing I know – God is here.
God is here, God is here.
One thing I know – God is here.

Words and music by David Haas.
Copyright © 2004 GIA Publications, Inc.
Used with permission. All rights reserved.

The Word of God

Zechariah 9:11, 14, 16–17; 10:1, 6–7b
Adapted by David Haas

Reader 1 These words are adapted from the Book of Zechariah.

Reader 2 All of you who are imprisoned by your fear, your *pride*, your *arrogance*, and your *lack of faith:*

Reader 1 Listen to me,
for this very day *hope* is in your midst,
for you will be restored,
and God will make it up for you twice over.

All God will bring us home.

Reader 2 God will appear over you,
and the trumpet will sound.
On that day,
God will save us all.

Reader 1 For we belong to God's flock;
for like the *jewels found in a crown,*
we will shine on the land of the one who calls us each by name.

Reader 2 What beauty comes from God!
For the wheat will make young men flourish, and the new wine will bring new life to young women.

All God will bring us home.

Reader 1 Ask God for the *spring rain,*
and we will receive showers of rain, giving life to all things.

Reader 2 God will strengthen us all,
showing compassion.

Reader 1 All who are young
will receive this gift and rejoice!
Their hearts will give thanks to God!

Reader 2 These words are from God and the servants of God.

All We give thanks to God
for the gift of this Word.
May we follow Christ
and deepen our call to faith.

Pause for silent reflection.

Song of Reflection

Leader At this time, let us listen to a song of reflection, which recalls God's presence in our lives.

Song is chosen from one of the following:

– You Are Mine *(CD 1, Track 18)*
– I Am For You *(CD 1, Track 19)*
– Turn My Heart, O God *(CD 1, Track 20)*

QUESTIONS FOR REFLECTION & FAITH SHARING

- *Where do I need to seek restoration? With my family or friends? In my relationship with God? Within myself?*

- *Where in my life do I need to move on, to receive healing?*

Listen or sing/pray along as the song is played. ———

INTERCESSIONS

Leader Let us now place our prayers before God.

We pray for us all, God's people in need of healing, and conversion, of a new beginning in our life of faith and service to each other.

We pray:

All Lord, hear our prayer.

Leader We pray for all who lead:
all those who make decisions for our world
and for our future.

We pray:

All Lord, hear our prayer.

Leader We pray for those who cannot move on,
who need the healing touch of God
in their lives.

We pray:

All Lord, hear our prayer.

Leader We pray for those who are close to us,
and for all who may be suffering in any way.

We pray:

Participants can name those for whom they want to pray.

All Lord, hear our prayer.

Leader We pray for any other needs
that we may have at this time.

Participants offer any prayers that they may have. At the conclusion of their prayers, the leader continues.

For all of these prayers and for those
that lie deep within our hearts.

We pray:

All Lord, hear our prayer.

THE LORD'S PRAYER

Leader   Gracious and awesome God,
we know that you are with us here,
and we see your presence
in your reconciling love –
reaching out to forgive, to heal,
and to welcome us into your arms
time and time again.

We remember your compassion,
as we come before you again,
broken and in need of healing.

So we offer and surrender ourselves
to your guidance in our lives
as we pray:

All   Our Father,
who art in heaven,
hallowed be thy name;
thy kingdom come;
thy will be done on earth
as it is in heaven.
Give us this day our daily bread;
and forgive us our trespasses
as we forgive those
who trespass against us;
and lead us not into temptation,
but deliver us from evil.
For the kingdom,
the power and the glory are yours,
now and forever. Amen.

May the Road Rise to Meet You *(CD 1, Track 3)*

May the road rise to meet you.
May the wind be at your back.
May the sun shine warm upon
  your face, upon your face.
May the rain fall softly on
  your fields,
And until we meet again,
may you keep safe in the
gentle, loving arms of God.

Words and music by Lori True.

FINAL BLESSING/SIGN OF PEACE

Leader   Let us now all bless one another.

All raise their hands in blessing of one another.

Sing or recite the words to this blessing.

Leader   Let us now end this time of prayer
by sharing with each other a sign of peace and
friendship in Christ.

With YOU BY MY SIDE
A CELEBRATION OF GOD'S FIDELITY LEADING US HOME

OPENING

As the leader begins to speak, someone from the group comes forward to light the candle.

Leader As we begin this time of prayer,
we call forth the light of Christ
to enlighten us, to guide us, to challenge us.
May this light help all of us
to remember and celebrate that God is here.

Listen or sing along as the song is played.

INVITATION TO HEAR THE WORD OF GOD

Leader Gracious and awesome God,
we know that you are here.
Open our minds to listen well
and hear the wisdom you bring!

All Gracious and awesome God,
we know that you are here.
Open our lips to speak boldly
and proclaim your truth in love!

Leader Gracious and awesome God,
we know that you are here.
Open our hearts
to generously receive the gift of your Word!

All Gracious and awesome God,
we know that you are here.
Do not be silent!
Speak to us!

Leader Let us now hear and listen well,
to these passages from the Word of God.

Environment: In place should be a Bible, attractive in appearance, open and displayed on a table with a candle next to it.

God Is Here
(CD 1, Track 1)

God is here, God is here.
One thing I know – God is here.
God is here, God is here.
One thing I know – God is here.

*Words and msuic by David Haas.
Copyright © 2004 GIA Publications, Inc.
Used with permission. All rights reserved.*

THE WORD OF GOD

Psalm 23
Adapted by David Haas

Reader 1   These words are adapted
from Psalm 23

Reader 2   *You*, God, are my shepherd.

Reader 1   *You*, God, are my shepherd.

All   *You*, God, are my shepherd.

Reader 2   You, God, are my shepherd,
and there is *absolutely nothing* more
that I need.

Reader 1   You give me rest in green meadows.

Reader 2   You set me down near calm waters.

Reader 1   It is there where you accept
my tired spirit.

All   You, God, are my shepherd.

Reader 2   You guide me along the right path;
you are *true to your name.*

Reader 1   If I ever walk in the darkness of death,
I fear no trouble at all
with you by my side.

Reader 2   You comfort me always.

All   You, God, are my shepherd.

Reader 1   You prepare your table with me in mind
as my foes observe.

Reader 2   You anoint and soothe me with oil,
and my cup is *filled to the brim.*

Reader 1   *Goodness, truth, love,* and *kindness*
will be with me every day,
always, throughout my days.

Reader 2   I will live *forever* in your house.

All   You, God, are my shepherd.

Reader 1   These words are from God and the
servants of God.

All   We give thanks to God
for the gift of this Word.
May we follow Christ
and deepen our call to faith.

Pause for silent reflection.

SONG OF REFLECTION

Leader   At this time let us listen to a song of
reflection, which recalls God's
presence in our lives.

Song is chosen from one of the following:

– With You By My Side *(CD 2, Track 1)*
– We Choose Life *(CD 2, Track 2)*
– Shepherd Me, O God *(CD 2, Track 3)*

QUESTIONS FOR REFLECTION & FAITH SHARING

• *As we think about the future, what are our greatest fears and worries?*

• *How can we invite others to walk "by our side" and allow them into our lives to help "shepherd" us through the dark and difficult times?*

Listen or sing/pray along as the song is played.

Take, O Take Me As I Am
(CD 1, Track 2)

Take, O take me as I am;
summon out what I shall be;
set your seal upon my heart
and live in me.

INTERCESSIONS

Leader   Let us now place our prayers before God.

We pray for us all, all who worry about the future,
who seek a shepherd to guide us,
as we walk together in faith.

We pray:

All   Lord, hear our prayer.

Leader   We pray for all who lead: all those who make decisions
for our world and for our future.

We pray:

All   Lord, hear our prayer.

Leader   We pray for those who always seem to dwell
in darkness, death, and the sadness
of hunger, poverty, and suffering.

We pray:

All   Lord, hear our prayer.

Leader   We pray for those who are close to us,
and for all who may be suffering in any way.

Participants can name those for whom they want to pray.

We pray:

All   Lord, hear our prayer.

Leader   We pray for any other needs
that we may have at this time.

Participants offer any prayers that they may have. At the conclusion of their prayers, the leader continues.

For all of these prayers and for those that lie deep
within our hearts.

We pray:

All   Lord, hear our prayer.

THE LORD'S PRAYER

Leader Gracious and awesome God,
we know that you are with us here,
for you always guide us along
the right path.
We believe that you have called
each and every one of us
to be strong in faith,
remembering that you are always
at our sides.

When we remember how you shepherd us, we
remember that we belong to you.

So we offer and surrender ourselves
to your guidance in our lives
as we pray:

All Our Father,
who art in heaven,
hallowed be thy name;
thy kingdom come;
thy will be done on earth
as it is in heaven.
Give us this day our daily bread;
and forgive us our trespasses
as we forgive those
who trespass against us;
and lead us not into temptation,
but deliver us from evil.
For the kingdom,
the power and the glory are yours,
now and forever. Amen.

FINAL BLESSING/SIGN OF PEACE

Leader Let us now all bless one another.

All raise their hands in blessing of one another.

Sing or recite the words to this blessing.

Leader Let us now end this time of prayer
by sharing with each other
a sign of peace and friendship in Christ.

May the Road Rise to Meet You *(CD 1, Track 3)*

May the road rise to meet you.
May the wind be at your back.
May the sun shine warm upon
  your face, upon your face.
May the rain fall softly on
  your fields,
And until we meet again,
may you keep safe in the
gentle, loving arms of God.

In the Morning Let Us Sing
A Celebration of Morning Prayer

Environment: In place should be a Bible, attractive in appearance, open and displayed on a table with a candle next to it.

OPENING

As the leader begins to speak, someone from the group comes forward to light the candle.

Leader   As we begin this time of prayer,
we ask God to awaken us
to welcome this day.
And so we begin:
O God, open our lips.

And we shall proclaim your praise!

Listen or sing along as the song is played.

God Is Here
(CD 1, Track 1)

God is here, God is here.
One thing I know – God is here.
God is here, God is here.
One thing I know – God is here.

Words and music by David Haas.

MORNING PSALM / PSALM 63
INVITATION TO HEAR THE WORD OF GOD

Leader   Let us now pray the ancient words of the psalmist:
"As morning breaks, come now and be my strength."

As morning breaks, come now and be my strength.

Leader   O God, my soul thirsts for you, my body longs for you, like a dry and weary land without water.

May we gaze upon your face,
a holy vision of strength and glory.

Leader   O God, your love is better than anything,
better than life itself.
My voice is filled with praise for you.

We offer you our praise,
and we raise our hands in prayer to you.

Leader   O God, my soul is filled as I am at a rich banquet.

Our mouths proclaim your glory.

Leader   Let us now hear and listen well
to this passage from the Word of God.

THE WORD OF GOD

> Deuteronomy 6:4–9; 7:6
> *Adapted by David Haas*

Reader 1   These words are adapted from the Book of Deuteronomy.

Reader 2   *Hear, O Israel!*

Reader 1   *Hear, O Israel!*

Reader 2   The Lord, our God, is Lord alone!

All   The Lord, our God, is Lord alone!

Reader 1   You shall love the Lord your God with *everything you have!*

Reader 2   With *all your heart,* with *all your soul,* and with *all your strength!*

All   The Lord, our God, is Lord alone!

Reader 1   Let these words that you hear today be written *on your heart.*

Reader 2   Repeat them over and over again, to each other, to your children, and keep them *close* to everyone.

All   The Lord, our God, is Lord alone!

Reader 1   Keep them alive in your heart at rest in your house, in your walking, in your lying down, or when you rise.

All   The Lord, our God, is Lord alone!

Reader 2   Know now that you are a people *consecrated, made special* to the Lord your God;

Reader 1   It is you that God has *chosen to be intimate with.*

Reader 2   God's *chosen* people!

All   The Lord our God, is Lord alone!

Reader 2   These words are from God and the servants of God.

All   We give thanks to God for the gift of this Word. May we follow Christ and deepen our call to faith.

Pause for silent reflection.

SONG OF REFLECTION

Leader   At this time let us listen to the words of the following psalm, as we reflect upon God's presence in our lives.

Psalm is chosen from one of the following:

– Let Us Sing *(CD 2, Track 4)*
– I Thirst for You *(CD 2, Track 5)*
– They Who Do Justice *(CD 2, Track 6)*

QUESTIONS FOR REFLECTION & FAITH SHARING

• *As we begin this day, what do we need from God to face our challenges?*

Listen or sing/pray along as the song is played.

Take, O Take Me As I Am
(CD 1, Track 2)

Take, O take me as I am;
summon out what I shall be;
set your seal upon my heart
and live in me.

*Words and music by John Bell.
Copyright © 1995 Iona Community/
GIA Publications, Inc. Used with
permission. All rights reserved.*

INTERCESSIONS

Leader   Let us now place our prayers before God.

We pray for us all, God's holy and chosen people,
called to remember God's action in our lives
and to respond in service to each other.

We pray:

All   Lord, hear our prayer.

Leader   We pray for all who lead:
all those who make decisions for our world
and for our future.

We pray:

All   Lord, hear our prayer.

Leader   We pray for those who are in need,
who may find it difficult to make it through this day.

We pray:

All   Lord, hear our prayer.

Leader   We pray for those who are close to us,
and for all who may be suffering in any way.

*Participants can name those
for whom they want to pray.*

We pray:

All   Lord, hear our prayer.

Leader   We pray for any other needs
that we may have at this time.

*Participants offer any prayers
that they may have. At the
conclusion of their prayers,
the leader continues.*

For all of these prayers and for those
that lie deep within our hearts.

We pray:

All   Lord, hear our prayer.

THE LORD'S PRAYER

Leader   Gracious and awesome God,
you are the morning and evening of our lives.
Come now, and show us the light of Christ;
draw us close to this light
that we know strengthens us
this day and every day.

Let the dawn from on high break upon us,
and may all of our prayers be gathered into
one great prayer, as we pray:

All   Our Father,
who art in heaven,
hallowed be thy name;
thy kingdom come;
thy will be done on earth
as it is in heaven.
Give us this day our daily bread;
and forgive us our trespasses
as we forgive those
who trespass against us;
and lead us not into temptation,
but deliver us from evil.
For the kingdom,
the power and the glory are yours,
now and forever. Amen.

FINAL BLESSING/SIGN OF PEACE

Leader   Let us now all bless one another.

All raise their hands in blessing of one another.

Sing or recite the words to this blessing.

Leader   Let us now bless the Lord,
giving thanks
as we dedicate ourselves to God
by sharing with each other
a sign of peace and friendship in Christ.

May the Road Rise to Meet
You *(CD 1, Track 3)*

May the road rise to meet you.
May the wind be at your back.
May the sun shine warm upon
  your face, upon your face.
May the rain fall softly on
  your fields,
And until we meet again,
may you keep safe in the
gentle, loving arms of God.

Let MY PRAYER RISE TO YOU
A CELEBRATION OF EVENING PRAYER

OPENING

As the leader begins to speak, someone from the group comes forward to light the candle.

Leader   As we begin this time of prayer,
we ask God to be with us
as this day comes to a close.
And so we begin.

Light and peace in Jesus Christ our Lord!

All   Thanks be to God!

Listen or sing along as the song is played. ————

EVENING PSALM / PSALM 141
INVITATION TO HEAR THE WORD OF GOD

Leader   Let us now pray the ancient words of the psalmist:
"May our prayers rise to you like incense, O God."

All   May our prayers rise to you like incense, O God.

Leader   Please hurry, Lord! I plead with you,
receive my prayer like the rising of incense,
and my hands, too, will raise as an evening offering.

All   Our hands, too, will raise as an evening offering.

Leader   Lord, keep a watch over my words,
and help me to avoid speaking evil
of others or committing acts of harm.

All   Help us to not join in the wicked ways of others
or sit at the tables of gossip and evil.

Leader   Lord, I turn to you this evening.
In you I find safety.

All   In you I find safety.

Leader   Let us now hear and listen well
to these passages from the Word of God.

Environment: In place should be a Bible, attractive in appearance, open and displayed on a table with a candle next to it.

God Is Here
(CD 1, Track 1)

God is here, God is here.
One thing I know – God is here.
God is here, God is here.
One thing I know – God is here.

THE WORD OF GOD

Psalm 121
Adapted by David Haas

Reader 1   These words are from Psalm 121

Reader 2   If we reach toward and *gaze upon the mountains*, will they come to help us?

All   Our help comes *only from God*, the maker of heaven and earth.

Reader 1   May God, who is always awake and *always near*, keep us all from stumbling.

Reader 2   For God, our guardian, *never rests or sleeps.*

Reader 1   God continually shields us, protecting us *always*.

All   The sun shall *never* harm us by day, nor will the moon at night.

Reader 2   God keeps us safe from evil, *peaceful and secure.*

All   God watches over us from near and far, *now and always.*

Reader 2   These words are from God and the servants of God.

All   We give thanks to God for the gift of this Word. May we follow Christ and deepen our call to faith.

Pause for silent reflection.

SONG OF REFLECTION

Leader   At this time let us listen to the following psalm, as we reflect upon God's presence in our lives.

Song is chosen from one of the following:

– Like Burning Incense, O Lord *(CD 2, Track 7)*
– Let Us Go Rejoicing *(CD 2, Track 8)*
– Here I Am *(CD 2, Track 9)*

QUESTIONS FOR REFLECTION & FAITH SHARING

• As this day comes to a close, what do I want to offer to God?

Listen or sing/pray along as the song is played.

INTERCESSIONS

Leader	Let us now place our prayers before God.
	We pray for us all, dependent on the mercy of God, called to remember God's action in our lives and to respond in service to each other.
	We pray:
All	Lord, hear our prayer.
Leader	We pray for all who lead: all those who make decisions for our world and for our future.
	We pray:
All	Lord, hear our prayer.
Leader	We pray for those who are in need, who may go to bed tonight hungry, alone, anxious, or afraid.
	We pray:
All	Lord, hear our prayer.
Leader	We pray for those who are close to us, and for all who may be suffering in any way.
	We pray:
All	Lord, hear our prayer.
Leader	We pray for any other needs that we may have at this time.
	For all of these prayers and for those that lie deep within our hearts.
	We pray:
All	Lord, hear our prayer.

Take, O Take Me As I Am
(CD 1, Track 2)

Take, O take me as I am;
summon out what I shall be;
set your seal upon my heart
and live in me.

Participants can name those for whom they want to pray.

Participants offer any prayers that they may have. At the conclusion of their prayers, the leader continues.

THE LORD'S PRAYER

Leader   Gracious and awesome God,
you are the morning and evening of our lives.
Come now, and keep us safe in light of Christ,
and draw us close to this light,
which we know abides with us tonight,
and will greet us in the morning.

Let us welcome the night in peace,
and may all of our prayers be gathered into
one great prayer, as we pray:

All   Our Father,
who art in heaven,
hallowed be thy name;
thy kingdom come;
thy will be done on earth
as it is in heaven.
Give us this day our daily bread;
and forgive us our trespasses
as we forgive those
who trespass against us;
and lead us not into temptation,
but deliver us from evil.
For the kingdom,
the power and the glory are yours,
now and forever. Amen.

FINAL BLESSING/SIGN OF PEACE

Leader   Let us now all bless one another.

All raise their hands in blessing of one another.

Sing or recite the words to this blessing.

Leader   May almighty God
bless us and keep us
with Jesus, the only Son of God,
and the Holy Spirit,
who is the source of life.

May we greet this night,
dedicating ourselves to God
by sharing with each other
a sign of peace and friendship in Christ.

May the Road Rise to Meet
You *(CD 1, Track 3)*

May the road rise to meet you.
May the wind be at your back.
May the sun shine warm upon
  your face, upon your face.
May the rain fall softly on
  your fields,
And until we meet again,
may you keep safe in the
gentle, loving arms of God.

Make Us Worthy

A CELEBRATION TO MAKE STRAIGHT THE WAY

OPENING

As the leader begins to speak, someone from the group comes forward to light the candle.

Leader   As we begin this time of prayer,
we call forth the light of Christ –
a living sign of Emmanuel: "God with us."
May this light that we honor here
help us to always remember that God is with us,
the holy light that warms us in our fear.

Listen or sing along as the song is played.

INVITATION TO HEAR THE WORD OF GOD

Leader   Gracious and awesome God,
you are our "Emmanuel – God with us"!
Open our minds to listen well
and hear the wisdom you bring!

All   Gracious and awesome God,
you are our "Emmanuel – God with us"!
Open our lips to speak boldly
and proclaim your truth in love!

Leader   Gracious and awesome God,
you are our "Emmanuel – God with us"!
Open our hearts to generously receive
the gift of your Word!

All   Gracious and awesome God,
you are our "Emmanuel – God with us"!
Do not be silent!
Speak to us!

Leader   Let us now hear and listen well
to this passage from the Word of God.

Environment: In place should be a Bible, attractive in appearance, open and displayed on a table with a candle next to it.

Warm the Time of Winter
(CD 2, Track 10)

When the wind of winter blows,
bringing times of solitude,
fill the silent, icy night;
be our hearts' compassion.

　Holy Light, warm our night;
　warm the time of winter.
　Holy Light, warm our night;
　warm the time of winter.

When we shiver in despair,
when the chill of death comes near,
hold us, Spirit, calm our fear,
while the evening deepens.

When in days of fallen snow,
change confounds or love burns low,
from the ashes may there rise
phoenix of our growing.

Words by Ruth Duck and music by Lori True. Text and tune copyright © 1992, 2000 GIA Publications, Inc. Used with permission. All rights reserved.

THE WORD OF GOD

Isaiah 40:1–5, 9–11
Adapted by David Haas

Reader 1   These words come to us from the prophet Isaiah.

Reader 2   *Comfort...*

Reader 1   *Comfort...*

Reader 2   Give *comfort* to my people, says our God.

Reader 1   Speak *tenderly* to Jerusalem, and proclaim to her that her service is at an end.

All   All guilt is lifted.

Reader 2   A voice cries out in the wilderness:

Reader 1   Make *straight a highway for our God!*

Reader 2   Every valley shall be filled, and every mountain and hill will be *made low.* The rugged land shall be plain.

All   The glory of the Lord shall be *revealed,* and we shall all see it together; for *God has spoken.*

Reader 1   Go up to a high mountain!

Reader 2   Cry out with everything that you have, "*herald and trumpet of good news*"!

Reader 1   Fear not and say to everyone: "*Here* is your God!"

All   *Here* is your God!

Reader 2   The Lord God comes with power, ruling with a *strong arm.*

Reader 1   Like a shepherd, God *feeds us all.*

Reader 2   Make *straight* a highway for our God!

All   Make straight a highway for our God!

Reader 1   These words are from God and the servants of God.

All   We give thanks to God for the gift of this Word. May we follow Christ and deepen our call to faith.

SONG OF REFLECTION

Leader   At this time let us listen to a song of reflection, and ponder the coming of the Lord into our midst this year.

– Make Us Worthy *(CD 2, Track 11)*

QUESTIONS FOR REFLECTION & FAITH SHARING

• What do we need to "make straight" in our lives during this season of preparation and expectation?

• How can we make ourselves more worthy to welcome Christ in our lives?

Listen or sing/pray along as the song is played.

INTERCESSIONS

Take, O Take Me As I Am
(CD 1, Track 2)

Take, O take me as I am;
summon out what I shall be;
set your seal upon my heart
and live in me.

Words and music by John Bell. Copyright © 1995 Iona Community/ GIA Publications, Inc. Used with permission. All rights reserved.

Leader   Let us now place our prayers before God.

We pray for us all, the Body of Christ:
who wait in hope for God's kingdom
to be born in our midst.

We pray:

All   Lord, hear our prayer.

Leader   We pray for all who lead:
all those who make decisions for our world
and for our future.

We pray:

All   Lord, hear our prayer.

Leader   We pray for those
who are waiting for the Lord in their pain:
the poor, the hungry, the suffering, the afraid,
and all who long for hope.

We pray:

All   Lord, hear our prayer.

Leader   We pray for those who are close to us,
for all who may be suffering
in any way.

Participants can name those for whom they want to pray.

We pray:

All   Lord, hear our prayer.

Leader   We pray for any other needs
that we may have at this time.

Participants offer any prayers that they may have. At the conclusion of their prayers, the leader continues.

For all of these prayers and for those
that lie deep within our hearts.

We pray:

All   Lord, hear our prayer.

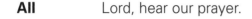

THE LORD'S PRAYER

Leader   Gracious and awesome God,
we know that you are with us here.
We believe that you have called
each and every one of us
to wait patiently for your coming again
and again in our lives and in our hearts.

We are ready to walk the journey of this season,
for we know that we belong to you.

So we offer and surrender ourselves
to your guidance in our lives
as we pray:

All   Our Father,
who art in heaven,
hallowed be thy name;
thy kingdom come;
thy will be done on earth
as it is in heaven.
Give us this day our daily bread;
and forgive us our trespasses
as we forgive those
who trespass against us;
and lead us not into temptation,
but deliver us from evil.
For the kingdom,
the power and the glory are yours,
now and forever. Amen.

May the Road Rise to Meet You *(CD 1, Track 3)*

May the road rise to meet you.
May the wind be at your back.
May the sun shine warm upon
  your face, upon your face.
May the rain fall softly on
  your fields,
And until we meet again,
may you keep safe in the
gentle, loving arms of God.

FINAL BLESSING/SIGN OF PEACE

Leader   Let us now all bless one another.

All raise their hands in blessing of one another.

Sing or recite the words to this blessing.

Leader   Let us now end this time of prayer
by sharing with each other
a sign of peace and friendship in Christ.

Great JOY

A CELEBRATION OF THE LIGHT OF NEW BIRTH

OPENING

As the leader begins to speak, someone from the group comes forward to light the candle.

Leader   As we begin this time of prayer, we call forth the light of Christ – a living sign of the Christ child born to us. May this light that we honor here help us to always remember the awesome gift of Christ Jesus – here among us now!

Listen or sing along as the song is played. ——

INVITATION TO HEAR THE WORD OF GOD

Leader   Gracious and awesome God,
you are here – born in us again!
Open our minds to listen well
and hear the wisdom you bring!

All   Gracious and awesome God,
you are here – born in us again!
Open our lips to speak boldly
and proclaim your truth in love!

Leader   Gracious and awesome God,
you are here – born in us again!
Open our hearts
to generously receive the gift of your Word!

All   Gracious and awesome God,
you are here – born in us again!
Do not be silent!
Speak to us!

Leader   Let us now hear and listen well
to these passages from the Word of God.

Environment: In place should be a Bible, attractive in appearance, open and displayed on a table with a candle next to it.

Great Joy
(CD 2, Track 12)

Great light in darkness!
Great light in darkness!
Great joy! Great joy!
Great joy! Great joy! Great joy!
A child is born
and there shall be peace.
Alleluia!

THE WORD OF GOD

Isaiah 9:1-6	
Adapted by David Haas	

Reader 1   These words are adapted from the prophet Isaiah.

Reader 2   The people who *walked in darkness…*

Reader 1   In *darkness…*

All   In *darkness…*

Reader 2   We have seen a great light!

Reader 1   A light has shone in the *land of gloom.*

Reader 2   For a child is born!

All   A child is born!

Reader 1   A son is given to us,
and upon his shoulder glory rests.

Reader 2   His names will be many:

Reader 1   *Wonder-Counselor!*

Reader 2   *God-Hero!*

Reader 1   *Divine and Eternal Presence!*

All   *Prince of Peace!*

Reader 2   His power is *vast and wide,
filled with peace.*

Reader 1   God will always confirm and *sustain*
good judgment and justice forever.

All   Our God of earth and heaven
will do this!

Reader 2   These words are from God and the servants of God.

All   We give thanks to God
for the gift of this Word.
May we follow Christ
and deepen our call to faith.

Pause for silent reflection.

SONG OF REFLECTION

Leader   At this time let us listen to a song of reflection, calling upon Jesus, our Christ and our brother, to come and be born in us this day.

Song is chosen from one of the following:
– The Encounter (CD 2, Track 13)
– Carol of the Child (CD 2, Track 14)

QUESTIONS FOR REFLECTION & FAITH SHARING

• *What name or image would we add to Isaiah's list of titles of the one born among us? Why?*

• *What light of this season do we hope to help shine brightly?*

Listen or sing/pray along as the song is played.

INTERCESSIONS

Take, O Take Me As I Am
(CD 1, Track 2)

Take, O take me as I am;
summon out what I shall be;
set your seal upon my heart
and live in me.

Words and music by John Bell.

Leader   Let us now place our prayers before God.

We pray for us all, the Body of Christ:
alive and new in the presence of Christ.

We pray:

All   Lord, hear our prayer.

Leader   We pray for all who lead:
all those who make decisions for our world
and for our future.

We pray:

All   Lord, hear our prayer.

Leader   We pray for those
who ache for new birth and new hope:
the old and the young who are alone,
the poor, the lonely, and those who suffer
from sadness and depression.

We pray:

All   Lord, hear our prayer.

Leader   We pray for those who are close to us,
for all who may be suffering in any way.

We pray:

*Participants can name those
for whom they want to pray.*

All   Lord, hear our prayer.

Leader   We pray for any other needs
that we may have at this time.

For all of these prayers and for those
that lie deep within our hearts.

*Participants offer any prayers
that they may have. At the
conclusion of their prayers,
the leader continues.*

We pray:

All   Lord, hear our prayer.

THE LORD'S PRAYER

Leader   Gracious and awesome God,
we know that you are with us here.
We believe that you have called
each and every one of us
to be born again,
to be your greatest gift to the world.

We are eager to celebrate the joy and hope of this
time, for we know that we belong to you.

So we offer and surrender ourselves
to your guidance in our lives
as we pray:

All   Our Father,
who art in heaven,
hallowed be thy name;
thy kingdom come;
thy will be done on earth
as it is in heaven.
Give us this day our daily bread;
and forgive us our trespasses
as we forgive those
who trespass against us;
and lead us not into temptation,
but deliver us from evil.
For the kingdom,
the power and the glory are yours,
now and forever. Amen.

FINAL BLESSING/SIGN OF PEACE

Leader   Let us now all bless one another.

All raise their hands in blessing of one another.

Sing or recite the words to this blessing.

Leader   Let us now end this time of prayer
by sharing with each other
a sign of peace and friendship in Christ.

May the Road Rise to Meet
You *(CD 1, Track 3)*

May the road rise to meet you.
May the wind be at your back.
May the sun shine warm upon
  your face, upon your face.
May the rain fall softly on
  your fields,
And until we meet again,
may you keep safe in the
gentle, loving arms of God.

Return TO THE LORD
A CELEBRATION OF CONVERSION TO CHRIST

OPENING

As the leader begins to speak, someone from the group comes forward to light the candle.

Leader
As we begin this time of prayer,
we call forth the light of Christ –
a living sign of our need for forgiveness and mercy,
a mercy found only in the unconditional love of Christ.
Let us now turn to the living God.

Listen or sing along as the song is played.

INVITATION TO HEAR THE WORD OF GOD

Leader
Gracious and awesome God,
you are the source of all forgiveness and mercy.
Open our minds to listen well
and hear the wisdom you bring!

All
Gracious and awesome God,
you are the living water that brings us to new life.
Open our lips to speak boldly
and proclaim your truth in love!

Leader
Gracious and awesome God,
you are the voice that calls us to renewal.
Open our hearts
to generously receive the gift of your Word!

All
Gracious and awesome God,
you are justice and peace for our troubled world.
Do not be silent!
Speak to us!

Leader
Let us now hear and listen well,
to these passages from the Word of God.

Environment: In place should be a Bible, attractive in appearance, open and displayed on a table with a candle next to it.

Return to the Lord
(CD 2, Track 16)

Return, return to the Lord,
your God.
Return, return to the Lord,
your God.

Who is gracious and merciful, and
slow to anger, abounding in love.

Words and music by David Haas.
Copyright © 2003 GIA Publication, Inc.
Used with permission. All rights reserved.

THE WORD OF GOD

Joel 2:12–18
Adapted by David Haas

Reader 1 These words are adapted from the prophet Joel.

Reader 2 Even *now*…

Reader 1 Even *now*…

All Even *now*…

Reader 2 Even *now*, says the Lord, *return to me with the entirety of your heart*, with fasting, mourning, and tears.

Reader 1 Tear your hearts, *not* the clothes that you are wearing.

Reader 2 *Return* to the Lord.

Reader 1 *Return* to the Lord.

All *Return* to the Lord.

Reader 2 God is *gracious* and *full of mercy.*

Reader 1 God is *slow to anger* and rich in kindness, relenting in punishment.

Reader 2 *Blow* the trumpet!

Reader 1 *Proclaim* a fast!

All Call the assembly together!

Reader 2 Gather *everyone,* notify the congregation, assemble the older ones, and *bring together* the children and infants.

Reader 1 Let all who serve the Lord weep and say: "*Spare your people, O Lord.*"

Reader 2 Why should anyone ask, "Where is our God?"

All The way of *compassion* and *mercy* is the way of God.

Reader 1 These words are from God and the servants of God.

All We give thanks to God for the gift of this Word. May we follow Christ and deepen our call to faith.

Pause for silent reflection.

SONG OF REFLECTION

Leader At this time let us listen to a song of reflection and call upon Jesus, who calls us to change and conversion.

Song is chosen from one of the following:
– I Am Standing Waiting (CD 2, Track 16)
– The Harvest of Justice (CD 2, Track 17)

QUESTIONS FOR REFLECTION & FAITH SHARING

- *If this season is truly a time to "return" and refocus, where in my life do I need to take a second look?*

- *Who is God for me during this time of self-inventory?*

Listen or sing along as the song is played. ————

INTERCESSIONS

Leader   Let us now place our prayers before God.

    We pray for us all, the Body of Christ:
All of us who are in need of forgiveness and healing.

We pray:

All   Lord, hear our prayer.

Leader   We pray for all who lead:
all those who make decisions for our world
and for our future.

We pray:

All   Lord, hear our prayer.

Leader   We pray for those
who are on the journey of conversion –
those seeking initiation,
those seeking forgiveness,
and all of us who seek renewal.

We pray:

All   Lord, hear our prayer.

Leader   We pray for those who are close to us,
for all who may be suffering in any way.

We pray:

Participants can name those for whom they want to pray.

All   Lord, hear our prayer.

Leader   We pray for any other needs
that we may have at this time.

    For all of these prayers and for those
that lie deep within our hearts.

Participants offer any prayers that they may have. At the conclusion of their prayers, the leader continues.

We pray:

All   Lord, hear our prayer.

THE LORD'S PRAYER

Leader Gracious and awesome God,
     we know that you are with us here.
     We believe that you have called
     each and every one of us
     to be whole again,
     to return to you
     with hearts full of compassion,
     mercy, justice, and peace.

     We are humbled by your awesome love for us,
     and we promise to respond in faith,
     for we know that we belong to you.

     So we offer and surrender ourselves
     to your guidance in our lives
     as we pray:

All   Our Father,
     who art in heaven,
     hallowed be thy name;
     thy kingdom come;
     thy will be done on earth
     as it is in heaven.
     Give us this day our daily bread;
     and forgive us our trespasses
     as we forgive those
     who trespass against us;
     and lead us not into temptation,
     but deliver us from evil.
     For the kingdom,
     the power and the glory are yours,
     now and forever. Amen.

FINAL BLESSING/SIGN OF PEACE

Leader Let us now all bless one another.

All raise their hands in blessing of one another.

Sing or recite the words to this blessing.

Leader Let us now end this time of prayer
     by sharing with each other
     a sign of peace and friendship in Christ.

May the Road Rise to Meet You *(CD 1, Track 3)*

May the road rise to meet you.
May the wind be at your back.
May the sun shine warm upon
 your face, upon your face.
May the rain fall softly on
 your fields,
And until we meet again,
may you keep safe in the
gentle, loving arms of God.

Come AND See

A CELEBRATION OF A NEW DAY IN CHRIST

OPENING

As the leader begins to speak, someone from the group comes forward to light the candle.

Leader As we begin this time of prayer,
we call forth the light of Christ –
a living sign of life in the midst of death,
of hope in the midst of hopelessness,
of rising again, again, and again!

Listen or sing as the song is played.

INVITATION TO HEAR THE WORD OF GOD

Leader Gracious and awesome God,
you are risen in us – now and forever!
Open our minds to listen well
and hear the wisdom you bring!

All Gracious and awesome God,
you are risen in us – now and forever!
Open our lips to speak boldly
and proclaim your truth in love!

Leader Gracious and awesome God,
you are risen in us – now and forever!
Open our hearts
to generously receive the gift of your Word!

All Gracious and awesome God,
you are risen in us – now and forever!
Do not be silent!
Speak to us!

Leader Let us now hear and listen well,
to these passages from the Word of God.

Environment: In place should be a Bible, attractive in appearance, open and displayed on a table with a candle next to it.

Come and See

(CD 2, Track 18)

We came there desp'rately,
so hopeless and afraid,
until we found the place
where Jesus Christ was laid.
Our sorrow and our fear
were banished on that glorious day.
The tomb was empty
and the stone was rolled away!

Come and see!
See what the Lord has done for you.
Come believe!
Out of our death comes life anew.
He is raised!
He has washed all our sins away.
Lift your praise!
Jesus has conquered on this day.

Some stumble on the way
in blindness and in sin.
Some find the open door
but fear to enter in.
It doesn't matter how, or who,
or when, or where, or why.
All who believe and love
shall never ever die!

Christ is our Lord and King!
O death, where is your sting?

Go out to all the world
and shout the blessed news.
Our lives have been made whole
by Christ, the faith we choose.
All chains are broken now,
and those enslaved are all set free.
All people lift your hearts
and join the jubilee!

Words and music by Michael Mahler.
Copyright © 2004 GIA Publications, Inc.
Used with permission. All rights reserved.

The Word of God

Psalm 118
Adapted by David Haas

Reader 1 These words are taken from
Psalm 118.

Reader 2 This *is* the day…

Reader 1 The day….

All This *is* the day that the Lord has made!
Let us rejoice!

Reader 2 Everyone give thanks!
God's love is *forever*!

Reader 1 Let Israel say:
God's love is *forever*!

Reader 2 Let all who honor the Lord say:
God's love is *forever*!

All God's love is forever!

Reader 1 The right hand of God is raised high!

Reader 2 Raised high, striking out with force!

Reader 1 We shall not die – *we will live!*

All *We will live!*

Reader 2 We shall not die,
but *we will live to tell of God's
wonderful deeds!*

Reader 1 The stone which others have rejected,
is *now the cornerstone!*

Reader 2 This is the *work of the Lord!*

All The work of the Lord!

Reader 1 *Wonderful!*

Reader 2 *Wonderful!*

All *Wonderful in our eyes!*

Reader 1 These words are from God
and the servants of God.

All We give thanks to God
for the gift of this Word.
May we follow Christ
and deepen our call to faith.

Pause for silent reflection.

Song of Reflection

Leader At this time let us listen to a song of
reflection and rejoice with the risen
Lord, whose tomb is empty,
and who has freed us all from the
bondage of fear and darkness.
Let us rejoice – for this is the day
the Lord has made!

Song is chosen from one of the following:

– Alleluia! Let Us Rejoice *(CD 2, Track 19)*
– God Has Done Marvelous Things *(CD 2, Track 20)*

QUESTIONS FOR REFLECTION & FAITH SHARING

• *How am I rising with Christ this Easter?*

• *How can I make my life truly an expression of hope in the Resurrection?*

Listen or sing along as the song is played.

Take, O Take Me As I Am
(CD 1, Track 2)

Take, O take me as I am;
summon out what I shall be;
set your seal upon my heart
and live in me.

INTERCESSIONS

Leader Let us now place our prayers before God.

We pray for us all, the Body of Christ:
All of us who are called to open up tombs
and be people of the Resurrection.

We pray:

All Lord, hear our prayer.

Leader We pray for all who lead: all those who make decisions
for our world and for our future.

We pray:

All Lord, hear our prayer.

Leader We pray for those
who find it difficult to accept the risen Christ,
who find it difficult to find resurrection
in the midst of their pain and suffering.

We pray:

All Lord, hear our prayer.

Leader We pray for those who are close to us,
for all who may be suffering
in any way.

*Participants can name those
for whom they want to pray.*

We pray:

All Lord, hear our prayer.

Leader We pray for any other needs
that we may have at this time.

*Participants offer any prayers
that they may have. At the
conclusion of their prayers,
the leader continues.*

For all of these prayers and for those
that lie deep within our hearts.

We pray:

All Lord, hear our prayer.

THE LORD'S PRAYER

Leader   Gracious and awesome God,
we know that you are with us here.
We believe that you have called
each and every one of us
to be alive again in your presence.

We rejoice in our new life;
we give thanks to you,
for we know that we belong to you.

So we offer and surrender ourselves
to your guidance in our lives
as we pray:

All   Our Father,
who art in heaven,
hallowed be thy name;
thy kingdom come;
thy will be done on earth
as it is in heaven.
Give us this day our daily bread;
and forgive us our trespasses
as we forgive those
who trespass against us;
and lead us not into temptation,
but deliver us from evil.
For the kingdom,
the power and the glory are yours,
now and forever. Amen.

FINAL BLESSING/SIGN OF PEACE

Leader   Let us now all bless one another.

All raise their hands in blessing of one another.

Sing or recite the words to this blessing.

Leader   Let us now end this time of prayer
by sharing with each other
a sign of peace and friendship in Christ.

May the Road Rise to Meet
You *(CD 1, Track 3)*

May the road rise to meet you.
May the wind be at your back.
May the sun shine warm upon
  your face, upon your face.
May the rain fall softly on
  your fields,
And until we meet again,
may you keep safe in the
gentle, loving arms of God.

SONGS OF REFLECTION

Deep Within
(CD 1, Track 4)

Deep within I will plant my law,
not on stone, but in your heart.
Follow me, I will bring you back,
you will be my own, and I will be your God.

I will give you a new heart, a new spirit within you,
for I will be your strength.

Return to me, with all your heart,
and I will bring you back.

I Lift My Soul
(CD 1, Track 5)

I lift my soul to you, O Lord.
To you I lift my hands,
I lift my heart, my soul.
I lift my soul to you, O Lord.
To you I lift my hands,
I lift my heart, my soul.

Lord, make me know your ways,
keep me on your path.
Walk with me in your truth and teach me.
You save my life, you are my song.

Your ways are good and just.
You find the lost,
you lead the humble to righteousness.
You help the poor to find the way.

We Praise You
(CD 1, Track 6)

We praise you, O Lord,
for all your works are wonderful.
We praise you, O Lord,
forever is your love.

Your wisdom made the heavens and the earth, O Lord;
You formed the land then set the lights;
And like your love the sun will rule the day,
And stars will grace the night.

You have chosen Jacob for yourself, O Lord;
So tenderly you spoke his name;
Then called a holy nation, Israel,
To make them yours, you came.

You Are the Presence
(CD 1, Track 7)

You are the presence,
breath of all passion and fire!
Filling the earth,
splashing the heavens with light!
Wind and the ocean,
maker of earth and the skies!
Color and sound,
seeking and singing the song!

You are the healing,
hope for all people in fear!
Comfort and peace,
tenderness is your embrace!
Word and the silence,
strength to the broken and weak!
Laughter from tears,
promise of life from death!

You are the thunder,
power and voice of the just!
Holy and strong,
fountain of wonder and might!
Father and mother,
lover and dreamer for all!
Joy of our lives,
returning, renewing the earth!

The Hand of God
(CD 1, Track 8)

The hand of God feeds us,
heals us, the hand of God!

All your works praise you,
your faithful ones bless you!
Let all proclaim your glory,
your power, your kingdom!

All eyes look to you,
you feed us in due season.
You come with open hands
to feed your creation!

You are just in all things,
loving and holy.
You are near to all who call your name,
who cry out in love and truth!

Words and music by David Haas.
Copyright © 2001 GIA Publications, Inc.
Used with permission. All rights reserved.

Who Is the Alien?
(CD 1, Track 9)

We were the alien; we were the outcast.
Captive in Egypt, our parents were slaves.
We knew the anguish and then the deliverance,
freed by our Maker, whose mighty hand saves!

Who is the alien? Who is the outcast?
Who is the hungry one barred from the feast?
Who is the widow, the slave, and the orphan?
These are our neighbors: the last and the least.

Different in practice and patterns of loving,
partnered in ways that seem strange to our own:
these are the outcasts we bar from the table,
failing to witness the grace we were shown.

Women and others our labels belittle,
people whose bodies bear limits of skill:
these are the outcasts whose gifts we discourage,
closing our hearts to God's open-armed will.

Christ is the outcast who calls to the table,
stretching his arms from the cross to enfold
sisters and brothers, alike in God's image,
breaking his body to make us all whole.

Who is the alien? Who is the outcast?
Who do we cast aside with foolish pride?

We must decide to walk beside.
Let none divide, let all abide.
We must provide a place at the table.

Words by Mary Louise Bringle and music and additional text
by Lori True. Copyright © 2002, 2005 GIA Publications, Inc.
Used with permission. All rights reserved.

You Will Find Me in Your Heart
(CD 1, Track 10)

I know the way I've planned for you;
filled with a future and with hope.
When you call on me I will hear you,
and you will find me in your heart.

If you seek me with your heart,
you will find me by your side.
I will restore your fortune and treasure,
and gather you from places lost.

After a time has drifted by,
I will come to visit you.
True to my promise, I'll bring you back,
and you will find a home again.

When you call and pray to me,
I will listen to your cry.
You will seek me in your longing,
and I'll be found, and we'll be one.

Words and music by David Haas.
Copyright © 1995 GIA Publications, Inc.
Used with permission. All rights reserved.

Everlasting Grace Is Yours
(CD 1, Track 11)

Filled with thanks we sing to God,
Everlasting grace is yours!
God who is the answer to our dreams,
Everlasting grace is yours!
God alone is wonderful and mighty,
Everlasting grace is yours!
Heaven and earth created in wisdom,
Everlasting grace is yours!

Alleluia, Alleluia! Everlasting grace is yours!
Alleluia, Alleluia! Everlasting grace is yours!

Stretching the earth around the water,
Everlasting grace is yours!
Burning bright with shining radiance,
Everlasting grace is yours!
Ruling the day with brilliant splendor,
Everlasting grace is yours!

Guarding the night with moon and starlight,
Everlasting grace is yours!

Striking down the tyrants of Egypt,
Everlasting grace is yours!
Freeing us from the terror of prison,
Everlasting grace is yours!
Op'ning wide the Red Sea waters,
Everlasting grace is yours!
Bring us through to life and freedom,
Everlasting grace is yours!

Leading us through raging torrents,
Everlasting grace is yours!
Tossing the armies deep into the sea,
Everlasting grace is yours!
Striking down the power of the mighty,
Everlasting grace is yours!
Saving us from all oppression,
Everlasting grace is yours!

We Praise You

(CD 1, Track 12)

For your sun that brightens the day: We praise you, Lord!
For your moon that guides the night: We praise you, Lord!
For your source of light and breath: We praise you, Lord!
For your song of death to life: We praise you, Lord!

> We praise you, Lord! You hear our cry!
> We praise you, Lord! You are the answer!
> We praise you, Lord! You are always near!
> With all our being we praise you, Lord!

For the treasure of joy and laughter: We praise you, Lord!
For the myst'ry of sorrow and tears: We praise you, Lord!
For the gift of love and healing: We praise you, Lord!
For the awesome pow'r of prayer: We praise you, Lord!

For your love that greets the morning: We praise you, Lord!
For your faithfulness through night:
> We praise you, Lord!
For your voice that sings in all of us: We praise you, Lord!
For your call to love and serve: We praise you, Lord!

For your Word, your Holy Wisdom: We praise you, Lord!
For the bread, the work of our hands: We praise you, Lord!
For the wine, the cup of blessing: We praise you, Lord!
For us all, your sacred presence: We praise you, Lord!

Oh, Lordy-O!

(CD 1, Track 13)

Oh, Lordy-O! Oh, Lordy-O!
Oh, Lordy-O! Oh, Lordy-O!

Everybody sing to the Lord of life; Oh, Lordy-O!
Sing to the God of all power and might. Oh, Lordy-O!
God of the mountain, God of the plain; Oh, Lordy-O!
God of the desert, God of the rain. Oh, Lordy-O!

> Oh, Lordy-O, Lord, Lord,
> sing praise to the Lord.
> Sing praises to God's name.
> Oh, Lordy-O, Lord, Lord,
> sing praise to the Lord.
> Sing praises to our God!

Oh, Lordy-O! Oh, Lordy-O!
Oh, Lordy-O! Oh, Lordy-O!

Sing me of spirit, sing me of heart; Oh, Lordy-O!
Sing me of freedom that flows without part. Oh, Lordy-O!
Sing me of justice, sing me of peace; Oh, Lordy-O!
Sing me of healing that brings a release. Oh, Lordy-O!

Oh, Lordy-O! Oh, Lordy-O!
Oh, Lordy-O! Oh, Lordy-O!

Who is the one that parts the sea? Oh, Lordy-O!
Who has created everything? Oh, Lordy-O!
God of the heavens, God of the earth; Oh, Lordy-O!
God of the people, God of new birth. Oh, Lordy-O!

Lord, It Is Good

(CD 1, Track 14)

> Lord, it is good to give thanks to you.
> Lord, it is good to give thanks to you,
> to praise your name,
> to praise your name.

How good to thank you, Lord, to praise your name,
   Most High,
To sing your love at dawn, your faithfulness at dusk
With sound of lyre and harp, with music of the lute.
For your work brings delight, your deeds invite song.

I marvel at what you do. Lord, how deep your thought!
Fools do not grasp this, nor the senseless understand.
Scoundrels spring up like the grass,
    flourish and quickly wither.
You, Lord, stand firm forever.

See how your enemies perish, scattered to the winds,
While you give me brute strength, pouring rich oil
    upon me.
I have faced my enemies, heard them plot against me.
The just shall grow like palm trees, majestic like cedars.

Refrain and music by David Haas.
Text for verses copyright © 1994, The International Committee on
English in the Liturgy, Inc. Used with permission. All rights reserved.
Music copyright © 1997 GIA Publications, Inc.
Used with permission. All rights reserved.

We Are Called

(CD 1, Track 15)

Come! Live in the light!
Shine with the joy and the love of the Lord!
We are called to be light for the kingdom,
to live in the freedom of the city of God!

    We are called to act with justice,
    we are called to love tenderly,
    we are called to serve one another;
    to walk humbly with God.

Come! Open your heart!
Show your mercy to all those in fear!
We are called to be hope for the hopeless
so all hatred and blindness will be no more!

Sing! Sing a new song!
Sing of that great day when all will be one!
God will reign, and we'll walk with each other
as sisters and brothers united in love!

Words and music by David Haas.
Copyright © 1988 GIA Publication, Inc.
Used with permission. All rights reserved.

Share Your Bread with the Hungry

(CD 1, Track 16)

Clothe the naked and take them to your care;
do not turn your back on your own.
Then your light shall break forth like the dawn,
and your wounds will be bound and healed.

    If you share your bread with the hungry,
    if you welcome the poor to your home,
    then your light will shine,
    your light will shine,
    and the sun will rise once more.

And your dignity shall go forth before you,
and the glory of God shall keep you safe.
Then you shall call and God will answer,
you will cry and God will be there.

If you remove all oppression from your midst,
and the shame of those who do you harm,
If you offer your bread to the hungry,
your God will dwell with you.

Words and music by David Haas.
Copyright © 1997 GIA Publications, Inc.
Used with permission. All rights reserved.

Show Me the Path

(CD 1, Track 17)

    Show me the path for my life;
    my portion and cup,
    it is you that I claim as my prize.

In you, O God, I take refuge.
I sing: "You are my God,"
In you alone I find joy,
you are the path of life.

I bless you, my God and my guide,
who leads my heart in the night.
I keep you, God, in my sight,
with you we stand in the light.

In you my soul will rejoice.
Even my body shall rest,
you will not leave me for dead,
your loved ones will be kept safe.

Words and music by David Haas.
Copyright © 1993 GIA Publications, Inc.
Used with permission. All rights reserved.

You Are Mine

(CD 1, Track 18)

I will come to you in the silence,
I will lift you from all your fear.
You will hear my voice, I claim you as my choice,
be still and know I am here.

I am hope for all who are hopeless,
I am eyes for all who long to see.
In the shadows of the night, I will be your light,
come and rest in me.

Do not be afraid, I am with you.
I have called you each by name.
Come and follow me,
I will bring you home;
I love you and you are mine.

I am strength for all the despairing,
healing for the ones who dwell in shame.
All the blind will see, the lame will all run free,
and all will know my name.

I am the Word that leads all to freedom,
I am the peace the world cannot give.
I will call your name, embracing all your pain,
stand up, now walk, and live!

I Am for You

(CD 1, Track 19)

There is a mountain, there is a sea.
There is a wind within all breathing.
There is an arm to break ev'ry chain,
There is a fire in all things living.
There is a voice that speaks from the flame:
"I am for you, I am for you, I am for you is my name."

There was a woman small as a star,
Full of the patient dreams of her nation,
Welcoming in an angel of God,
Welcoming in God's bold invitation.
"Let it be done," she sang, "unto me.
I am for you, I am for you, I am for you: let it be."

There was a man who walked in the storm,
Caught in between the waves and the lightning,
Sharing his bread with those cast aside,
Healing by touch the lost and the dying.
Sending us forth, he says to his friends:
"I am for you, I am for you, I am for you to the end."

We are anointed, servants of God;
We have been born again of Spirit.
We are the word God speaks to the world,
Freedom and light to all who will hear it.
So let us be the Word of the Lord:
I am for you, I am for you, I am for you evermore.

There is a world that waits in the womb;
There is a hope unborn God is bearing,
Though the powers of death prowl the night,
There is a day our God is preparing.
Sing 'round the fire to waken the dawn:
I am for you, I am for you, I am for you: We are one.

Turn My Heart, O God

(CD 1, Track 20)

Turn my heart, O God.
Turn my heart, O God.
Take my pain and brokenness;
shape my life for you.
Come and turn my heart, O God.

From all that leads to death, to seek the way of life:
Come and turn my heart, O God.
From all that leads to sin, to holiness and grace:
Come and turn my heart, O God.
From all despair and grief, to hope of life renewed:
Come and turn my heart, O God.

From bitterness and hate, to tenderness and care:
Come and turn my heart, O God.
From selfishness and greed, to gen'rous caring love:
Come and turn my heart, O God.
From all deceit and lies, to faithfulness and truth:
Come and turn my heart, O God.

O let your Spirit come and cleanse my inmost heart:
Come and turn my heart, O God.
Give back to me the joy of walking in your way:
Come and turn my heart, O God.
O fill me with your grace that I might sing your praise:
Come and turn my heart, O God.

O bring me home to you, Most Holy, Blessed One:
Come and turn my heart, O God.
And let my spirit rest within your loving heart:
Come and turn my heart, O God.
For you alone can raise my weary soul to life:
Come and turn my heart, O God.

With You By My Side

(CD 2, Track 1)

When I'm feeling all alone,
and I'm far away from home,
God, I need you to hear me.
When my friends all turn away,
then I ache to hear you say
that you are with me through it all.

You are the light,
you're the song that I'm singing;
whom should I fear when you are with me?
For you are my God,
and with you there is nothing I can't do,
with you by my side.

When I feel all sick inside,
with no safe place to hide,
God, I need you to listen.
When it seems I can't go on,
then I long to hear the song
reminding me you are my friend.

And as I go through my life,
I will keep you in my sight
to walk with me and be my strength.
God, I know your plan for me:
to help all those in need.
To you alone I give my life!

Words and music by David Haas.
Copyright © 1998 GIA Publications, Inc.
Used with permission. All rights reserved.

We Choose Life

(CD 2, Track 2)

Why do you stand on the hill and gaze up above?
The choice lies before you
and waits for you to decide!
I place before you life and death;
choose life and you will be free!

We choose life! Life for each other!
Sister and brother,
answer the call to rise from death!
We choose life! Alleluia, alleluia!

Do not walk on the shore and look to the sea!
The answer lies not in the waves,
but deep in your soul!
I place before you life and death;
choose life and you will be free!

Do not harden your heart, but walk in my way.
Forgive as I forgive,
and live in the light!
I place before you life and death;
choose life and you will be free!

Words and music by David Haas.
Copyright © 1997 GIA Publications, Inc.
Used with permission. All rights reserved.

Shepherd Me, O God

(CD 2, Track 3)

Shepherd me, O God,
beyond my wants, beyond my fears,
from death into life.

God is my shepherd, so nothing shall I want,
I rest in the meadows of faithfulness and love,
I walk by the quiet waters of peace.

Gently you raise me and heal my weary soul,
you lead me by pathways of righteousness and truth,
my spirit shall sing the music of your name.

Though I should wander the valley of death,
I fear no evil, for you are at my side,
your rod and your staff, my comfort and my hope.

You have set me a banquet of love in the face of hatred,
crowning me with love beyond my pow'r to hold.

Surely your kindness and mercy follow me
all the days of my life;
I will dwell in the house of my God for evermore.

Words and music by Marty Haugen.
Copyright © 1986 GIA Publications, Inc.
Used with permission. All rights reserved.

Let Us Sing

(CD 2, Track 4)

In the morning let us sing, let us sing praise to you.
Let us sing glad songs of praise to you.

O God, you are my God, for you I long;
for you my soul is thirsting.
My body pines for you
like a dry, weary land without water.
I gaze on you in the sanctuary
to see your strength and your glory.

For your love is better than life,
my lips will speak your praise.
I will bless you all my life,
in your name I will lift up my hands.
My soul shall be filled as with a banquet,
my mouth shall praise you with joy.

On my bed I remember you.
On you I muse through the night
for you have been my help;
in the shadow of your wings I rejoice.
My soul clings to you;
your right hand holds me fast.

I Thirst for You

(CD 2, Track 5)

As a deer craves running water,
I thirst for you, my God;
I thirst for God, the living God.
When will I see your face?

Send your light and truth.
They will escort me to the holy mountain
where you make your home.

I will approach the altar of God,
God, my highest joy,
and praise you with the harp,
God, my God.

Why are you sad, my heart?
Why do you grieve?
Wait, wait for the Lord.
I will yet praise God my savior.

They Who Do Justice

(CD 2, Track 6)

They who do justice will live in the presence of God!
They who do justice will live in the presence of God!

Those who walk blamelessly and live their lives
    doing justice,
who keep the truth in their heart, and slander not with
    their tongue!

Who harm not another, nor take up reproach to
    their neighbor,
who hate the sight of the wicked, but honor the
    people of God!

Who show no condition in sharing the gifts of
    their treasure,
who live not off the poor: They will stand firm forever!

Like Burning Incense, O Lord

(CD 2, Track 7)

Like burning incense, O Lord,
let my prayer rise to you.

I call out to you, come quickly to my aid.
My song cries out to you, O listen to me now.
I raise my hands in off'ring to you.

Let me speak your truth; watch over all I say.
Keep my thoughts on you; let goodness rule my heart.
Keep me far from those who do harm.

Never let me dine with those who seek to harm.
Keep your holy ones always at my side.
Plant your wisdom deep in my soul.

I look to you for help; I seek your loving eyes.
Guard my life for you; spare me from all wrong.
Keep all evil far from my heart.

Glory be to God and to God's only Son,
glory to the Spirit, three in one,
now and forever. Amen.

Let Us Go Rejoicing

(CD 2, Track 8)

Let us go rejoicing to the house of the Lord,
to the house of the Lord.

I rejoiced because they said to me,
we will go up to the house of the Lord.
And now we have set foot within your gates,
O Jerusalem.

We've come to praise the Lord's name
as he ordered Israel.
Here are the courts, the courts of justice,
the royal courts of David.

Since all are my brothers and sisters,
I say peace, peace be with you all.
Since God our Father, our Father lives here,
we pray for your happiness.

Words and music by Leon C. Roberts.
Copyright © 1981, 1997 GIA Publications, Inc.
Used with permission. All rights reserved.

Here I Am

(CD 2, Track 9)

> Here I am, here I am, I come to do your will.
> Here I am, here I am, I come to do your will.

I waited for God, who bent down to hear me.
God put a new song in my mouth, a hymn of praise!

You did not seek offerings or sacrifice.
You opened my eyes to see, my ears to hear.
Yes, I will come to do your will!

I proclaim your greatness, Lord, to all those around me.
My lips are not sealed, never holding back the story.
You know this is true, I come to do your will!

Words and music by Tony Alonso.
Copyright © 2004 GIA Publications, Inc.
Used with permission. All rights reserved.

Make Us Worthy

(CD 2, Track 11)

> Lord, make us worthy.
> Make us worthy to see your face.
> Fill us with your word, O Lord,
> and heal us with your grace.

Open up your tender arms
for your lost ones have come home.
Let the sprinkling of your joyful tears
wash us clean again.

You are strength when we are weak.
You are warmth when we are cold.
You are light for those in darkness.
You are hope for all.

Fashion ploughshares from our swords.
Rip the hatred from our minds.
Help us choose your paths of justice.
Bless us all with peace.

Words and music by Michael Mahler.
Copyright © 2003 GIA Publications, Inc.
Used with permission. All rights reserved.

The Encounter

(CD 2, Track 13)

Where shepherds lately knelt,
and kept the angel's word,
I come in half-belief,
a pilgrim strangely stirred;
but there is room
and welcome there for me.

In that unlikely place
I find him as they said:
sweet new born Babe, how frail!
And in a manger bed:
a still small Voice
to cry one day for me.

How should I not have known
Isaiah would be there,
his prophecies fulfilled?
With pounding heart, I stare:
a Child, a Son,
the Prince of Peace – for me.

Can I, will I forget
how Love was born
and burned its way into my heart –
unasked, unforced, unearned,
to die, to live,
and not alone for me?

Words ("Where Shepherds Lately Knelt") by Jaroslav J. Vajda
and music by David Haas. Text copyright © 1986 Concordia Publis
House. Used with permission. Music copyright © 2001 GIA
Publications, Inc. Used with permission. All rights reserved.

Carol of the Child

(CD 2, Track 14)

No eye has seen, nor ear has ever heard;
Joy beyond joy, a message from God's Word!
Go and proclaim now to all the land,
The reign of our God is close at hand!
Look for the gift born to us in a stall!
For here a little child will lead us all!

From the sword, a plowshare will be found,
Nations will lay their weapons on the ground!
Peace once hidden is now in our sight:
People of God, come and walk in the light!
Welcome the gift born to us in a stall!
For here a little child will lead us all!

On that day all hate and war will end,
Wolf and lamb will call each other "friend."
Flowers will bud forth, ready to bloom,
Greeting the Lord, yes, soon, very soon!
Come see the gift born to us in a stall!
For here a little child will lead us all!

Say to all frightened hearts, our God is here!
Coming with strength for all who live in fear!
Healing the blind one and freeing the slave,
Here comes your God who is longing to save!
Honor the gift born to us in a stall!
For here a little child will lead us all!

Make straight the path, do not delay!
Come and prepare all people for God's way!
Ev'ry valley, mountain and hill,
Ev'ry pure heart for God's love to fill!
Share the gift born to us in a stall,
For here a little child will lead us all!
This holy child will lead us all!

I Am Standing Waiting

(CD 2, Track 16)

I am standing waiting, waiting at your door,
one of hunger's children from a billion poor,
though you cannot see me, though I am so small –
listen to my crying, crying for us all.

I stand at your table asking to be fed,
holding up my rice bowl, begging for your bread,
I stand at your schoolroom longing just to learn,
hoping that you'll teach me ways to live and earn.

I stand at your clinic begging for vaccine,
I stand at your wash place where the water's clean,
I stand at your office, beg the Heads of State,
I am just a child, so I must hope and wait.

I stand at your churches, listen to your prayers,
long to know a God who understands and cares.
If there is a God, a God who loves the poor,
I'm still standing waiting, waiting at your door.

The Harvest of Justice

(CD 2, Track 17)

May we find richness in the harvest of justice
which Christ Jesus has ripened for us.
Bread for the journey, bread for the hungry,
all for the glory and praise of God.

Gather with patience for those who have nothing.
Leave them your riches, and you will receive.
Make room for the poor ones, make way for the stranger;
for I am the Lord, the Lord your God.

For to have mercy on those forgotten,
this is my true law, this is my command:
Clothe the naked, be home for the orphan,
be hope for the widow, and welcome the lost.

Alleluia! Let Us Rejoice

(CD 2, Track 19)

Alleluia! Alleluia!
Alleluia! Alleluia!

This is the day the Lord has made,
let us rejoice, be glad, and sing!
Thanks and praise be to our God,
for his mercy endures forevermore!

The right hand of God has come with power,
the Lord, our God, is lifted high!
I shall not die, but I shall live
and rejoice in the works of the Lord!

The stone which the builders once denied
now has become the cornerstone.
By the Lord has this been done,
it has brought wonder to our eyes!

God Has Done Marvelous Things

(CD 2, Track 20)

Earth and all stars! Loud rushing planets,
Sing to the Lord a new song!
O, victory! Loud shouting army,
Sing to the Lord a new song!

God has done marvelous things,
I too, I too sing praises with a new song!
God has done marvelous things,
I too, I too sing praises with a new song!

Hail, wind, and rain! Loud blowing snowstorm,
Sing to the Lord a new song!
Flowers and trees! Loud rustling dry leaves,
Sing to the Lord a new song!

Trumpet and pipes! Loud clashing cymbals,
Sing to the Lord a new song!
Harp, lute and lyre! Loud humming cellos,
Sing to the Lord a new song!

Engines and steel! Loud pounding hammers,
Sing to the Lord a new song!
Limestone and beams! Loud building workers,
Sing to the Lord a new song!

Classrooms and labs! Loud boiling test tubes,
Sing to the Lord a new song!
Athlete and band! Loud cheering people,
Sing to the Lord a new song!

Knowledge and truth! Loud sounding wisdom,
Sing to the Lord a new song!
Daughter and son! Loud praying members,
Sing to the Lord a new song!

TOPICAL INDEX OF PRAYER CELEBRATIONS AND SONGS

Acceptance

Prayer Celebrations
All Your Works Are Wonderful, 19
I Will Bring You Home, 35
I Will Plant My Law, 15
Who Is the Alien?, 23
With You By My Side, 39
You Are Always Near, 27

Songs
God Is Here (CD 1, Track 1)
Hand of God, The (CD 1, Track 8)
Here I Am (CD 2, Track 9)
I Am For You (CD 1, Track 19)
Shepherd Me, O God (CD 2, Track 3)
Take, O Take Me As I Am
    (CD 1, Track 2)
Who Is the Alien? (CD 1, Track 9)
With You By My Side (CD 2, Track 1)
You Are Mine (CD 1, Track 18)
You Will Find Me in Your Heart
    (CD 1, Track 10)

Advent

Prayer Celebration
Make Us Worthy, 51

Songs
I Lift My Soul (CD 1, Track 5)
Let Us Go Rejoicing (CD 2, Track 8)
Make Us Worthy (CD 2, Track 11)
Warm the Time of Winter
    (CD 2, Track 10)

Anxiety and Stress

Prayer Celebrations
Come and See, 63
I Will Bring You Home, 35
Who Is the Alien?, 23
With You By My Side, 39
You Are Always Near, 27

Songs
Deep Within (CD 1, Track 4)
Hand of God, The (CD 1, Track 8)
I Am for You (CD 1, Track 19)
I Thirst for You (CD 2, Track 5)
May the Road Rise to Meet You
    (CD 1, Track 3)
Shepherd Me, O God
    (CD 2, Track 3)
Take, O Take Me As I Am
    (CD 1, Track 2)
With You By My Side (CD 2, Track 1)
You Are Mine (CD 1, Track 18)
You Will Find Me in Your Heart
    (CD 1, Track 10)

Belief

Prayer Celebrations
I Will Plant My Law, 15
You Are Always Near, 27

Songs
Deep Within (CD 1, Track 4)
Here I Am (CD 2, Track 9)
Lord, It Is Good (CD 1, Track 14)
Make Us Worthy (CD 2, Track 11)
Show Me the Path (CD 1, Track 17)
They Who Do Justice (CD 2, Track 6)
We Are Called (CD 1, Track 15)
We Choose Life (CD 2, Track 2)

Calm

Prayer Celebrations
I Will Bring You Home, 35
With You By My Side, 39
You Are Always Near, 27

Songs
Deep Within (CD 1, Track 4)
I Lift My Soul (CD 1, Track 5)
With You By My Side (CD 2, Track 1)
You Are Mine (CD 1, Track 18)
You Will Find Me in Your Heart
    (CD 1, Track 10)

Challenge

Prayer Celebrations
Come and See, 63
I Will Plant My Law, 15
Make Us Worthy, 51
Return to the Lord, 59
Walk Humbly with God, 31
Who Is the Alien?, 23
With You By My Side, 39

Songs
Come and See (CD 2, Track 18)
Harvest of Justice, The
    (CD 2, Track 17)
Here I Am (CD 2, Track 9)
I Am Standing Waiting (CD 2, Track 16)

Make Us Worthy (CD 2, Track 11)
Return to the Lord (CD 2, Track 15)
Share Your Bread with the Hungry
    (CD 1, Track 16)
Show Me the Path (CD 1, Track 17)
They Who Do Justice (CD 2, Track 6)
We Are Called (CD 1, Track 15)
We Choose Life (CD 2, Track 2)
Who Is the Alien? (CD 1, Track 9)

Christmas

Prayer Celebration
Great Joy, 55

Songs
Carol of the Child (CD 2, Track 14)
Encounter, The (CD 2, Track 13)
God Is Here (CD 1, Track 1)
Great Joy (CD 2, Track 12)

Comfort and Recovery

Prayer Celebrations
Come and See, 63
I Will Bring You Home, 35
Who Is the Alien?, 23
With You By My Side, 39
You Are Always Near, 27

Songs
God Has Done Marvelous Things
    (CD 2, Track 20)
God Is Here (CD 1, Track 1)
Hand of God, The (CD 1, Track 8)
I Am for You (CD 1, Track 19)
I Lift My Soul (CD 1, Track 5)
I Thirst for You (CD 2, Track 5)
May the Road Rise to Meet You
    (CD 1, Track 3)
Shepherd Me, O God
    (CD 2, Track 3)
Show Me the Path (CD 1, Track 17)
Turn My Heart, O God (CD 1, Track
    20)
We Choose Life (CD 2, Track 2)
With You By My Side (CD 2, Track 1)
You Are Mine (CD 1, Track 18)

Commitment

Prayer Celebrations
I Will Plant My Law, 15
Return to the Lord, 59
Walk Humbly with God, 31
With You By My Side, 39
You Are Always Near, 27

You Are the Presence (CD 1, Track 7)

Empowering Others

Prayer Celebrations
Walk Humbly with God, 31
Who Is the Alien?, 23
With You By My Side, 39
You Are Always Near, 27

Songs
God Has Done Marvelous Things
    (CD 2, Track 20)
Harvest of Justice, The (CD 2, Track 17)
Let Us Go Rejoicing (CD 2, Track 8)
Shepherd Me, O God (CD 2, Track 3)
Share Your Bread with the Hungry
    (CD 1, Track 16)
They Who Do Justice (CD 2, Track 6)
We Are Called (CD 1, Track 15)
Who Is the Alien? (CD 1, Track 9)
With You By My Side (CD 2, Track 1)

Evening

Prayer Celebration
Let My Prayer Rise to You, 47

Songs
Deep Within (CD 1, Track 4)
Here I Am (CD 2, Track 9)
I Lift My Soul (CD 1, Track 5)
Let Us Go Rejoicing (CD 2, Track 8)
Like Like Burning Incense, O Lord
    (CD 2, Track 7)
Return to the Lord (CD 2, Track 15)
Show Me the Path (CD 1, Track 17)
Take, O Take Me As I Am
    (CD 1, Track 2)
Warm the Time of Winter
    (CD 2, Track 10)

Faith

Prayer Celebrations
Come and See, 63
I Will Plant My Law, 15
Make Us Worthy, 51
Return to the Lord, 59
Walk Humbly with God, 31
With You By My Side, 39
You Are Always Near, 27

Songs
Come and See (CD 2, Track 18)
God Has Done Marvelous Things
    (CD 2, Track 20)
God Is Here (CD 1, Track 1)

Hand of God, The (CD 1, Track 8)
I Am for You (CD 1, Track 19)
I Lift My Soul (CD 1, Track 5)
Let Us Go Rejoicing (CD 2, Track 8)
Lord, It Is Good (CD 1, Track 14)
May the Road Rise to Meet You
    (CD 1, Track 3)
Shepherd Me, O God (CD 2, Track 3)
Return to the Lord (CD 2, Track 15)
Show Me the Path (CD 1, Track 17)
Take, O Take Me As I Am
    (CD 1, Track 2)
We Are Called (CD 1, Track 15)
We Praise You (Haas) (CD 1, Track
    12)
With You By My Side (CD 2, Track 1)
You Are Mine (CD 1, Track 18)
You Are the Presence (CD 1, Track 7)

Family and Community

Prayer Celebrations
All Your Works Are Wonderful, 19
Come and See, 63
I Will Bring You Home, 35
In the Morning Let Us Sing, 43
Make Us Worthy, 51
Return to the Lord, 59
Walk Humbly with God, 31
With You By My Side, 39
You Are Always Near, 27

Songs
Come and See (CD 2, Track 18)
God Has Done Marvelous Things
    (CD 2, Track 20)
God Is Here (CD 1, Track 1)
Great Joy (CD 2, Track 12)
Hand of God, The (CD 1, Track 8)
Let Us Go Rejoicing (CD 2, Track 8)
Lord, It Is Good (CD 1, Track 14)
Take, O Take Me As I Am
    (CD 1, Track 2)
We Are Called (CD 1, Track 15)
We Praise You (Haas) (CD 1, Track
    12)
Who Is the Alien? (CD 1, Track 9)
With You By My Side (CD 2, Track 1)
You Are Mine (CD 1, Track 18)
You Will Find Me in Your Heart
    (CD 1, Track 10)

Fear

Prayer Celebrations
I Will Plant My Law, 15
With You By My Side, 39

You Are Always Near, 27

Songs
Come and See (CD 2, Track 18)
God Has Done Marvelous Things
    (CD 2, Track 20)
God Is Here (CD 1, Track 1)
Hand of God, The (CD 1, Track 8)
I Am For You (CD 1, Track 19)
I Thirst for You (CD 2, Track 5)
Return to the Lord (CD 2, Track 15)
Shepherd Me, O God (CD 2, Track 3)
Show Me the Path (CD 1, Track 17)
Take, O Take Me As I Am
    (CD 1, Track 2)
Who Is the Alien? (CD 1, Track 9)
With You By My Side (CD 2, Track 1)
You Are Mine (CD 1, Track 18)

Following God

Prayer Celebrations
Come and See, 63
I Will Plant My Law, 15
In the Morning Let Us Sing, 43
Return to the Lord, 59
Walk Humbly with God, 31
With You By My Side, 39
You Are Always Near, 27

Songs
Come and See (CD 2, Track 18)
Hand of God, The (CD 1, Track 8)
Here I Am (CD 2, Track 9)
I Lift My Soul (CD 1, Track 5)
Let Us Go Rejoicing (CD 2, Track 8)
Lord, It Is Good (CD 1, Track 14)
Make Us Worthy (CD 2, Track 11)
Shepherd Me, O God (CD 2, Track 3)
Return to the Lord (CD 2, Track 15)
Share Your Bread with the Hungry
    (CD 1, Track 16)
Show Me the Path (CD 1, Track 17)
Take, O Take Me As I Am
    (CD 1, Track 2)
We Are Called (CD 1, Track 15)

Forgiveness and Mercy

Prayer Celebrations
All Your Works Are Wonderful, 19
Come and See, 63
I Will Bring You Home, 35
Let My Prayer Rise to You, 47
Return to the Lord, 59
Who Is the Alien?, 23
With You By My Side, 39

You Are Always Near, 27

Songs
Everlasting Grace Is Yours
   (CD 1, Track 11)
I Lift My Soul (CD 1, Track 5)
Shepherd Me, O God (CD 2, Track 3)
Take, O Take Me As I Am
   (CD 1, Track 2)
Turn My Heart, O God (CD 1, Track
   20)
You Are Mine (CD 1, Track 18)

Freedom

Prayer Celebrations
Come and See, 63
Great Joy, 55
I Will Bring You Home, 35
I Will Plant My Law, 15
Walk Humbly with God, 31
Who Is the Alien?, 23
With You By My Side, 39
You Are Always Near, 27

Songs
Come and See (CD 2, Track 18)
Everlasting Grace Is Yours
   (CD 1, Track 11)
Hand of God, The (CD 1, Track 8)
Here I Am (CD 2, Track 9)
They Who Do Justice (CD 2, Track 6)
We Are Called (CD 1, Track 15)
We Choose Life (CD 2, Track 2)
You Will Find Me in Your Heart
   (CD 1, Track 10)

Generosity

Prayer Celebrations
All Your Works Are Wonderful, 19
Come and See, 63
In the Morning Let Us Sing, 43
With You By My Side, 39
You Are Always Near, 27

Songs
Come and See (CD 2, Track 18)
Everlasting Grace Is Yours
   (CD 1, Track 11)
God Has Done Marvelous Things
   (CD 2, Track 20)
God Is Here (CD 1, Track 1)
Great Joy (CD 2, Track 12)
Hand of God, The (CD 1, Track 8)
I Am for You (CD 1, Track 19)
I Lift My Soul (CD 1, Track 5)

Lord, It is Good (CD 1, Track 14)
Oh, Lordy O! (CD 1, Track 13)
We Praise You (Daigle, Ducote,
   Balhoff) (CD 1, Track 6)
We Praise You (Haas) (CD 1, Track 12)
You Are the Presence (CD 1, Track 7)

Giftedness

Prayer Celebrations
All Your Works Are Wonderful, 19
Great Joy, 55
In the Morning Let Us Sing, 43
With You By My Side, 39
You Are Always Near, 27

Songs
Everlasting Grace Is Yours
   (CD 1, Track 11)
God Has Done Marvelous Things
   (CD 2, Track 20)
God Is Here (CD 1, Track 1)
Let Us Sing (CD 2, Track 4)
Lord, It Is Good (CD 1, Track 14)
We Praise You (Daigle, Ducote,
   Balhoff) (CD 1, Track 6)

God's Blessing

Prayer Celebrations
All Your Works Are Wonderful, 19
Come and See, 63
Great Joy, 55
In the Morning Let Us Sing, 43
You Are Always Near, 27

Songs
Everlasting Grace Is Yours
   (CD 1, Track 11)
God Has Done Marvelous Things
   (CD 2, Track 20)
God Is Here (CD 1, Track 1)
Great Joy (CD 2, Track 12)
Hand of God, The (CD 1, Track 8)
I Am for You (CD 1, Track 19)
Lord, It Is Good (CD 1, Track 14)
May the Road Rise to Meet You
   (CD 1, Track 2)
Oh, Lordy O! (CD 1, Track 13)
We Praise You (Daigle, Ducote,
   Balhoff) (CD 1, Track 6)
We Praise You (Haas) (CD 1, Track 12)
With You By My Side (CD 2, Track 1)
You Are the Presence (CD 1, Track 7)

God's Friendship

Prayer Celebrations
All Your Works Are Wonderful, 19
Great Joy, 55
With You By My Side, 39
You Are Always Near, 27

Songs
God Has Done Marvelous Things
   (CD 2, Track 20)
God Is Here (CD 1, Track 1)
I Am for You (CD 1, Track 19)
I Lift My Soul (CD 1, Track 5)
Lord, It Is Good (CD 1, Track 14)
May the Road Rise to Meet You
   (CD 1, Track 3)
Take, O Take As I Am (CD 1, Track 2)
With You By My Side (CD 2, Track 1)
You Are Mine (CD 1, Track 18)
You Will Find Me in Your Heart
   (CD 1, Track 10)

God's Power

Prayer Celebrations
All Your Works Are Wonderful, 19
In the Morning Let Us Sing, 43
Walk Humbly with God, 31
You Are Always Near, 27

Songs
Come and See (CD 2, Track 18)
Everlasting Grace Is Yours (CD 1,
   Track 11)
God Has Done Marvelous Things
   (CD 2, Track 20)
Great Joy (CD 2, Track 12)
Hand of God, The (CD 1, Track 8)
I Am for You (CD 1, Track 19)
Let Us Go Rejoicing (CD 2, Track 8)
Oh, Lordy-O! (CD 1, Track 13)
Shepherd Me, O God (CD 2, Track 3)
They Who Do Justice (CD 2, Track 6)
You Are the Presence (CD 1, Track 7)

God's Protection

Prayer Celebrations
I Will Bring You Home, 35
Let My Prayer Rise to You, 47
With You By My Side, 39
You Are Always Near, 27

Songs
Everlasting Grace Is Yours
  (CD 1, Track 11)
God Has Done Marvelous Things
  (CD 2, Track 20)
God Is Here (CD 1, Track 1)
I Am for You (CD 1, Track 19)
I Lift My Soul (CD 1, Track 5)
May the Road Rise to Meet You
  (CD 1, Track 3)
With You By My Side (CD 2, Track 1)
You Are Mine (CD 1, Track 18)
You Will Find Me in Your Heart
  (CD 1, Track 10)

God's Tenderness

Prayer Celebrations
All Your Works Are Wonderful, 19
I Will Bring You Home, 35
Who Is the Alien?, 23
With You By My Side, 39
You Are Always Near, 27

Songs
God Is Here (CD 1, Track 1)
May the Road Rise to Meet You
  (CD 1, Track 3)
Shepherd Me, O God
  (CD 2, Track 3)
Take, O Take Me As I Am
  (CD 1, Track 2)
With You By My Side (CD 2, Track 1)
You Are Mine (CD 1, Track 18)
You Will Find Me in Your Heart
  (CD 1, Track 10)

God's Unconditional Love

Prayer Celebrations
Come and See, 63
Great Joy, 55
I Will Bring You Home, 35
With You By My Side, 39
You Are Always Near, 27

Songs
Carol of the Child (CD 2, Track 14)
Come and See (CD 2, Track 18)
Everlasting Grace Is Yours
  (CD 1, Track 11)
God Has Done Marvelous Things
  (CD 2, Track 20)
God Is Here (CD 1, Track 1)
Great Joy (CD 2, Track 12)
Hand of God, The (CD 1, Track 8)
I Am for You (CD 1, Track 19)

You Will Find Me in Your Heart
  (CD 1, Track 10)

God's Will

Prayer Celebrations
I Will Plant My Law, 15
Return to the Lord, 59
Walk Humbly with God, 31

Songs
Harvest of Justice, The (CD 2, Track 17)
Here I Am (CD 2, Track 9)
Let Us Go Rejoicing (CD 2, Track 8)
Make Us Worthy (CD 2, Track 11)
Return to the Lord (CD 2, Track 15)
Share Your Bread with the Hungry
  (CD 1, Track 16)
They Who Do Justice (CD 2, Track 6)
We Are Called (CD 1, Track 15)
Who Is the Alien? (CD 1, Track 9)

Growth

Prayer Celebrations
I Will Plant My Law, 15
Who Is the Alien?, 23
Walk Humbly with God, 31
With You By My Side, 39
Return to the Lrod, 59

Songs
Come and See (CD 2, Track 18)
Hand of God, The (CD 1, Track 8)
I Lift My Soul (CD 1, Track 5)
Let Us Go Rejoicing (CD 2, Track 8)
Make Us Worthy (CD 2, Track 11)
Return to the Lord (CD 2, Track 15)
Shepherd Me, O God (CD 2, Track 3)
Show Me the Path (CD 1, Track 17)
Take, O Take Me As I Am (CD 1,
  Track 2)
Turn My Heart, O God (CD 1, Track
  20)

Grief

Prayer Celebrations
Come and See, 63
I Will Bring You Home, 35
Let My Prayer Rise to You, 47
Return to the Lord, 59
Who Is the Alien?, 23
With You By My Side, 39
You Are Always Near, 27

Songs
Come and See (CD 2, Track 18)

I Am for You (CD 1, Track 19)
I Am Standing Waiting
  (CD 2, Track 16)
Shepherd Me, O God (CD 2, Track 3)
Take, O Take Me As I Am
  (CD 1, Track 2)
Who Is the Alien? (CD 1, Track 9)
With You By My Side (CD 2, Track 1)
You Are Mine (CD 1, Track 18)
You Will Find Me in Your Heart
  (CD 1, Track 10)

Guidance

Prayer Celebrations
I Will Plant My Law, 15
Make Us Worthy, 51
Return to the Lord, 59
Walk Humbly with God, 31
With You By My Side, 39

Songs
Deep Within (CD 1, Track 4)
Here I Am (CD 2, Track 9)
I Thirst for You (CD 2, Track 5)
Make Us Worthy (CD 2, Track 11)
Return to the Lord (CD 2, Track 15)
Shepherd Me, O God (CD 2, Track 3)
Show Me the Path (CD 1, Track 17)
With You By My Side (CD 2, Track 2)

Guilt and Shame

Prayer Celebrations
I Will Bring You Home, 35
Walk Humbly with God, 31
Who Is the Alien?, 23
With You By My Side, 39
You Are Always Near, 27

Songs
Come and See (CD 2, Track 18)
Make Us Worthy (CD 2, Track 11)
Take, O Take Me As I Am
  (CD 1, Track 2)
Turn My Heart, O God (CD 1, Track
  20)
We Are Called (CD 1, Track 15)
We Praise You (Haas) (CD 1, Track
  12)
Who Is the Alien? (CD 1, Track 9)
With You By My Side (CD 2, Track 1)
You Are Mine (CD 1, Track 18)

Happiness

Prayer Celebrations
All Your Works Are Wonderful, 19
Come and See, 63
Great Joy, 55
I Will Bring You Home, 35
I Will Plant My Law, 15
In the Morning Let Us Sing, 43
With You By My Side, 39
You Are Always Near, 27

Songs
Alleluia! Let Us Rejoice (CD 2, Track 19)
Come and See (CD 2, Track 18)
Deep Within (CD 1, Track 4)
God Is Here (CD 1, Track 1)
Great Joy (CD 2, Track 12)
Let Us Sing (CD 2, Track 4)
May the Road Rise to Meet You
    (CD 1, Track 2)
We Praise You (Daigle, Ducote,
    Balhoff) (CD 1, Track 6)
With You By My Side (CD 2, Track 1)
You Are Mine (CD 1, Track 18)

Holy Spirit

Prayer Celebrations
All Your Works Are Wonderful, 19
Come and See, 63
I Will Bring You Home, 35
I Will Plant My Law, 15
In the Morning Let Us Sing, 43
Let My Prayer Rise to You, 47
With You By My Side, 39

Songs
Come and See (CD 2, Track 18)
Deep Within (CD 1, Track 4)
We Praise You (Daigle, Ducote,
    Balhoff) (CD 1, Track 6)
With You By My Side (CD 2, Track 1)

Hope

Prayer Celebrations
All Your Works Are Wonderful, 19
Come and See, 63
Great Joy, 55
I Will Bring You Home, 35
Who Is the Alien?, 23
With You By My Side, 39
You Are Always Near, 27

Songs
Carol of the Child (CD 2, Track 14)
Come and See (CD 2, Track 18)

Deep Within (CD 1, Track 4)
God Has Done Marvelous Things
    (CD 2, Track 20)
God Is Here (CD 1, Track 1)
Great Joy (CD 2, Track 12)
Hand of God, The (CD 1, Track 8)
I Am For You (CD 1, Track 19)
Let Us Go Rejoicing (CD 2, Track 8)
Shepherd Me, O God (CD 2, Track 3)
Show Me the Path (CD 1, Track 17)
We Choose Life (CD 2, Track 2)
With You By My Side (CD 2, Track 1)
You Are Mine (CD 1, Track 18)
You Will Find Me in Your Heart
    (CD 1, Track 10)

Integrity

Prayer Celebrations
Come and See, 63
I Will Plant My Law, 15
Walk Humbly with God, 31
Who Is the Alien?, 23

Songs
Carol of the Child (CD 2, Track 14)
Deep Within (CD 1, Track 4)
Everlasting Grace Is Yours
    (CD 1, Track 11)
God Has Done Marvelous Things
    (CD 2, Track 20)
God Is Here (CD 1, Track 1)
Harvest of Justice, The (CD 2, Track 17)
Here I Am (CD 2, Track 9)
Make Us Worthy (CD 2, Track 11)
Share You Bread with the Hungry
    (CD 1, Track 16)
Show Me the Path (CD 1, Track 17)
They Who Do Justice (CD 2, Track 6)
We Are Called (CD 1, Track 15)
We Choose Life (CD 2, Track 2)

Knowing God

Prayer Celebrations
Come and See, 63
Great Joy, 55
I Will Bring You Home, 35
I Will Plant My Law, 15
Return to the Lord, 59
Walk Humbly with God, 31
Who Is the Alien?, 23
With You By My Side, 39
You Are Always Near, 27

Songs
Come and See (CD 2, Track 18)
God Is Here (CD 1, Track 1)
I Am for You (CD 1, Track 19)
I Thirst for You (CD 2, Track 5)
Let Us Go Rejoicing (CD 2, Track 8)
Return to the Lord (CD 2, Track 15)
Show Me the Path (CD 1, Track 17)
With You By My Side (CD 2, Track 1)
You Are Mine (CD 1, Track 18)
You Are the Presence (CD 1, Track 7)
You Will Find Me in Your Heart
    (CD 1, Track 10)

Lent

Prayer Celebration
Return to the Lord, 59

Songs
Deep Within (CD 1, Track 4)
Harvest of Justice, The (CD 2, Track 17)
Here I Am (CD 2, Track 9)
I Am Standing Waiting (CD 2, Track 16)
Return to the Lord (CD 2, Track 15)
Shepherd Me, O God (CD 2, Track 3)
Share Your Bread with the Hungry
    (CD 1, Track 16)
Take, O Take Me As I Am
    (CD 1, Track 2)
Turn My Heart, O God (CD 1, Track 20)
Who Is the Alien? (CD 1, Track 9)
You Are Mine (CD 1, Track 18)

Letting Go

Prayer Celebrations
Come and See, 63
I Will Bring You Home, 35
Let My Prayer Rise to You, 47
Return to the Lord, 59
With You By My Side, 39
You Are Always Near, 27

Songs
Here I Am (CD 2, Track 9)
I Lift My Soul (CD 1, Track 5)
I Thirst for You (CD 2, Track 5)
Return to the Lord (CD 2, Track 15)
Shepherd Me, O God (CD 2, Track 3)
Show Me the Path (CD 1, Track 17)
Take, O Take Me As I Am
    (CD 1, Track 2)
Turn My Heart, O God (CD 1, Track 20)

With You By My Side (CD 2, Track 1)
You Are Mine (CD 1, Track 18)

Listening to God

Prayer Celebrations
I Will Plant My Law, 15
Let My Prayer Rise to You, 47
Make Us Worthy, 51
Return to the Lord, 59
Walk Humbly with God, 31
You Are Always Near, 27

Songs
Hand of God, The (CD 1, Track 8)
Here I Am (CD 2, Track 9)
I Thirst for You (CD 2, Track 5)
Return to the Lord (CD 2, Track 15)
Show Me the Path (CD 1, Track 17)
Take, O Take Me As I Am
   (CD 1, Track 2)
Turn My Heart, O God (CD 1, Track
   20)
You Are Mine (CD 1, Track 18)
You Are the Presence (CD 1, Track 7)

Loneliness

Prayer Celebrations
All Your Works Are Wonderful, 19
You Are Always Near, 27
Walk Humbly with God, 31
I Will Bring You Home, 35
With You By My Side, 39

Songs
God Has Done Marvelous Things
   (CD 2, Track 20)
God Is Here (CD 1, Track 1)
I Am for You (CD 1, Track 19)
Let Us Sing (CD 2, Track 4)
With You By My Side (CD 2, Track 1)
You Are Mine (CD 1, Track 18)
You Are the Presence (CD 1, Track 7)
You Will Find Me in Your Heart
   (CD 1, Track 10)

Love of Self

Prayer Celebrations
All Your Works Are Wonderful, 19
With You By My Side, 39

Songs
Take, O Take Me As I Am
   (CD 1, Track 2)
I Am for You (CD 1, Track 19)

Meditation

Prayer Celebrations
All Your Works Are Wonderful, 19
I Will Bring You Home, 35
I Will Plant My Law, 15
In the Morning Let Us Sing, 43
Let My Prayer Rise to You, 47
Return to the Lord, 59
You Are Always Near, 27

Songs
God Is Here (CD 1, Track 1)
I Thirst for You (CD 2, Track 5)
Return to the Lord (CD 2, Track 15)
Take, O Take Me As I Am
   (CD 1, Track 2)
With You By My Side (CD 2, Track 1)
You Are Mine (CD 1, Track 18)
You Will Find Me in Your Heart
   (CD 1, Track 10)

Ministry

Prayer Celebrations
I Will Plant My Law, 15
Walk Humbly with God, 31
Who Is the Alien?, 23

Songs
Come and See (CD 2, Track 18)
Deep Within (CD 1, Track 4)
Here I Am (CD 2, Track 9)
Let Us Go Rejoicing (CD 2, Track 8)
Make Us Worthy (CD 2, Track 11)
Return to the Lord (CD 2, Track 15)
Share Your Bread with the Hungry
   (CD 1, Track 16)
Show Me the Path (CD 1, Track 17)
Take, O Take Me As I Am
   (CD 1, Track 1)
They Who Do Justice (CD 2, Track 6)
We Are Called (CD 1, Track 15)
We Choose Life (CD 2, Track 2)
Who Is the Alien? (CD 1, Track 9)
With You By My Side (CD 2, Track 1)

Morning

Prayer Celebration
In the Morning Let Us Sing, 43

Songs
Alleluia! Let Us Rejoice
   (CD 2, Track 19)
Come and See (CD 2, Track 18)
Everlasting Grace Is Yours
   (CD 1, Track 11)

God Has Done Marvelous Things
   (CD 2, Track 20)
God Is Here (CD 1, Track 1)
I Lift My Soul (CD 1, Track 5)
I Thirst for You (CD 2, Track 5)
Let Us Sing (CD 2, Track 4)
Lord, It Is Good (CD 1, Track 14)
May the Road Rise to Meet You
   (CD 1, Track 3)
Oh, Lordy O! (CD 1, Track 13)
Take, O Take Me As I Am
   (CD 1, Track 2)
They Who Do Justice (CD 2, Track 6)
We Praise You (Haas) (CD 1, Track 12)

Moving Forward

Prayer Celebrations:
Come and See, 63
I Will Bring You Home, 35
Return to the Lord, 59
Walk Humbly with God, 31
With You By My Side, 39

Songs:
Come and See (CD 2, Track 18)
Here I Am (CD 2, Track 9)
Show Me the Path (CD 1, Track 17)
They Who Do Justice (CD 2, Track 6)
Turn My Heart, O God (CD 1, Track
   20)
We Are Called (CD 1, Track 15)
With You By My Side (CD 2, Track 1)
You Are Mine (CD 1, Track 18)

Newness of Life

Prayer Celebrations:
Come and See, 63
Great Joy, 55
I Will Bring You Home, 35
In the Morning I Will Sing,
Return to the Lord, 59
Walk Humbly with God, 31
With You By My Side, 39
You Are Always Near, 27

Songs:
Alleluia! Let Us Rejoice
   (CD 2, Track 19)
Come and See (CD 2, Track 18)
Everlasting Grace Is Yours
   (CD 1, Track 11)
God Has Done Marvelous Things
   (CD 2, Track 20)
God Is Here (CD 1, Track 1)

Justice

Prayer Celebrations:
Great Joy, 55
I Will Plant My Law, 15
Walk Humbly with God, 31

Songs:
Carol of the Child (CD 2, Track 14)
Deep Within (CD 1, Track 4)
Great Joy (CD 2, Track 12)
Hand of God, The (CD 1, Track 8)
Harvest of Justice, The (CD 2, Track 17)
I Am Standing Waiting (CD 2, Track 16)
Let Us Go Rejoicing (CD 2, Track 8)
Share Your Bread with the Hungry
    (CD 1, Track 16)
Show Me the Path (CD 1, Track 17)
They Who Do Justice (CD 2, Track 6)
We Are Called (CD 1, Track 15)
We Choose Life (CD 2, Track 2)
Who Is the Alien? (CD 1, Track 9)

Relationship with God

Prayer Celebrations:
Return to the Lord, 59
Walk Humbly with God, 31
With You By My Side, 39
You Are Always Near, 27

Songs:
Deep Within (CD 1, Track 4)
Here I Am (CD 2, Track 9)
I Am for You (CD 1, Track 19)
I Thirst for You (CD 2, Track 5)
Return to the Lord (CD 2, Track 15)
Shepherd Me, O God (CD 2, Track 3)
Show Me the Path (CD 1, Track 17)
Take, O Take Me As I Am
    (CD 1, Track 2)
Turn My Heart, O God (CD 1, Track
    20)
With You By My Side (CD 2, Track 1)
You Are Mine (CD 1, Track 18)
You Are the Presence (CD 1, Track 7)
You Will Find Me in Your Heart
    (CD 1, Track 10)

Renewal

Prayer Celebrations:
Come and See, 63
I Will Bring You Home, 35
I Will Plant My Law, 15
In the Morning Let Us Sing, 43
Return to the Lord, 59

Walk Humbly with God, 31
With You By My Side, 39

Songs:
Come and See (CD 2, Track 18)
Deep Within (CD 1, Track 4)
Let Us Go Rejoicing (CD 2, Track 8)
Let Us Sing (CD 2, Track 4)
Return to the Lord (CD 2, Track 15)
Show Me the Path (CD 1, Track 17)
Turn My Heart, O God (CD 1, Track
    20)
We Are Called (CD 1, Track 15)
With You By My Side (CD 2, Track 1)
You Are Mine (CD 1, Track 18)

Responsibility

Prayer Celebrations:
I Will Plant My Law, 15
Return to the Lord, 59
Walk Humbly with God, 31
Who Is the Alien?, 23

Songs:
Carol of the Child (CD 2, Track 14)
Deep Within (CD 1, Track 4)
Harvest of Justice, The (CD 2, Track 17)
Share Your Bread with the Hungry
    (CD 1, Track 16)
They Who Do Justice (CD 2, Track 6)
Turn My Heart, O God (CD 1, Track
    20)
We Are Called (CD 1, Track 15)
Who Is the Alien? (CD 1, Track 9)

Resurrection

Prayer Celebrations:
All Your Works Are Wonderful, 19
Come and See, 63
I Will Bring You Home, 35
In the Morning Let Us Sing, 43
With You By My Side, 39
You Are Always Near, 27

Songs:
Alleluia! Let Us Rejoice
    (CD 2, Track 19)
Come and See (CD 2, Track 18)
Everlasting Grace Is Yours
    (CD 1, Track 11)
God Has Done Marvelous Things
    (CD 2, Track 20)
Let Us Sing (CD 2, Track 4)
Oh, Lordy O! (CD 1, Track 13)

We Choose Life (CD 2, Track 2)
We Praise You (Daigle, Ducote,
    Balhoff) (CD 1, Track 6)
We Praise You (Haas) (CD 1, Track 12)
You Are the Presence (CD 1, Track 7)

Service

Prayer Celebrations:
Come and See, 63
I Will Plant My Law, 15
Make Us Worthy, 51
Return to the Lord, 59
Walk Humbly with God, 31
Who Is the Alien?, 23
With You By My Side, 39

Songs:
Carol of the Child (CD 2, Track 14)
Deep Within (CD 1, Track 4)
Harvest of Justice, The (CD 2, Track 17)
Share Your Bread with the Hungry
    (CD 1, Track 16)
They Who Do Justice (CD 2, Track 6)
Turn My Heart, O God (CD 1, Track
    20)
We Are Called (CD 1, Track 15)
Who Is The Alien? (CD 1, Track 9)

Sickness and Suffering

Prayer Celebrations:
Come and See, 63
I Will Bring You Home, 35
Walk Humbly with God, 31
Who Is the Alien?, 23
With You By My Side, 39
You Are Always Near, 27

Songs:
Come and See (CD 2, Track 18)
God Is Here (CD 1, Track 1)
Hand of God, The (CD 1, Track 8)
I Am for You (CD 1, Track 19)
I Am Standing Waiting
    (CD 2, Track 16)
I Thirst for You (CD 2, Track 5)
May the Road Rise to Meet You
    (CD 1, Track 3)
Share Your Bread with the Hungry
    (CD 1, Track 16)
Shepherd Me, O God (CD 2, Track 3)
Take, O Take Me As I Am
    (CD 1, Track 2)
They Who Do Justice (CD 2, Track 6)
We Are Called (CD 1, Track 15)
We Choose Life (CD 2, Track 2)

Who Is the Alien? (CD 1, Track 9)
With You By My Side (CD 2, Track 1)
You Are Mine (CD 1, Track 18)

Strength

Prayer Celebrations:
I Will Bring You Home, 35
Walk Humbly with God, 31
With You By My Side, 39
You Are Always Near, 27

Songs:
Come and See (CD 2, Track 18)
God Is Here (CD 1, Track 1)
Hand of God, The (CD 1, Track 8)
I Am for You (CD 1, Track 19)
I Am Standing Waiting (CD 2, Track 16)
I Thirst for You (CD 2, Track 5)
May the Road Rise to Meet You
    (CD 1, Track 3)
Share Your Bread with the Hungry
    (CD 1, Track 16)
Shepherd Me, O God (CD 2, Track 3)
Take, O Take Me As I Am
    (CD 1, Track 2)
They Who Do Justice (CD 2, Track 6)
We Are Called (CD 1, Track 15)
We Choose Life (CD 2, Track 2)
Who Is the Alien? (CD 1, Track 9)
With You By My Side (CD 2, Track 1)
You Are Mine (CD 1, Track 18)

Surrender

Prayer Celebrations:
I Will Plant My Law, 15
Let My Prayer Rise to You, 47
Make Us Worthy, 51
Return to the Lord, 59
Walk Humbly with God, 31
With You By My Side, 39

Songs:
Deep Within (CD 1, Track 4)
God Is Here (CD 1, Track 1)
Hand of God, The (CD 1, Track 8)
Like Burning Incense, O Lord (CD 2,
    Track 7)
Make Us Worthy (CD 2, Track 11)
Return to the Lord (CD 2, Track 15)
Show Me the Path (CD 1, Track 17)
Take, O Take Me As I Am
    (CD 1, Track 2)
Turn My Heart, O God (CD 1, Track
    20)
With You By My Side (CD 2, Track 1)

You Are Mine (CD 1, Track 18)

Thanksgiving and Gratitude

Prayer Services:
All Your Works Are Wonderful, 19
Come and See, 63
Great Joy, 55
In the Morning Let Us Sing, 43
With You By My Side, 39
You Are Always Near, 27

Songs:
Alleluia! Let Us Rejoice
    (CD 2, Track 19)
Come and See (CD 2, Track 18)
Everlasting Grace Is Yours
    (CD 1, Track 11)
God Has Done Marvelous Things
    (CD 2, Track 20)
God Is Here (CD 1, Track 1)
Great Joy (CD 2, Track 12)
Hand of God, The (CD 1, Track 8)
Here I Am (CD 2, Track 9)
I Lift My Soul (CD 1, Track 5)
Lord, It Is Good (CD 1, Track 14)
Oh, Lordy O! (CD 1, Track 13)
We Praise You (Haas) (CD 1, Track 12)

Trust in God

Prayer Celebrations:
I Will Bring You Home, 35
I Will Plant My Law, 15
Walk Humbly with God, 31
With You By My Side, 39
You Are Always Near, 27

Songs:
Deep Within (CD 1, Track 4)
God Has Done Marvelous Things
    (CD 2, Track 20)
God Is Here (CD 1, Track 1)
Hand of God, The (CD 1, Track 8)
Here I Am (CD 2, Track 9)
I Am for You (CD 1, Track 19)
I Thirst for You (CD 2, Track 5)
Return to the Lord (CD 2, Track 15)
Shepherd Me, O God (CD 2, Track 3)
Show Me the Path (CD 1, Track 17)
Take, O Take Me As I Am
    (CD 1, Track 2)
Turn My Heart, O God (CD 1, Track
    20)
With You By My Side (CD 2, Track 1)
You Are Mine (CD 1, Track 18)

Truth

Prayer Celebrations:
All Your Works Are Wonderful, 19
Come and See, 63
I Will Plant My Law, 15

Songs:
Come and See (CD 2, Track 18)
Deep Within (CD 1, Track 4)
God Has Done Marvelous Things
    (CD 2, Track 20)
God Is Here (CD 1, Track 1)
Hand of God, The (CD 1, Track 8)
We Praise You (Daigle, Ducote,
    Balhoff) (CD 1, Track 6)
You Are the Presence (CD 1, Track 7)

Unity

Prayer Celebrations:
Come and See, 63
Great Joy, 55
I Will Plant My Law, 15
Return to the Lord, 59
Walk Humbly with God, 31
Who Is the Alien?, 23
With You By My Side, 39
You Are Always Near, 27

Songs:
Come and See (CD 2, Track 18)
Deep Within (CD 1, Track 4)
God Has Done Marvelous Things
    (CD 2, Track 20)
God Is Here (CD 1, Track 1)
Great Joy (CD 2, Track 12)
I Am for You (CD 1, Track 19)
Lord, It Is Good (CD 1, Track 14)
We Are Called (CD 1, Track 15)
We Praise You (Haas) (CD 1, Track 6)
Who Is the Alien? (CD 1, Track 9)
With You By My Side (CD 2, Track 1)
You Are Mine (CD 1, Track 18)

Waiting

Prayer Celebrations:
Let My Prayer Rise to You, 47
Make Us Worthy, 51
Return to the Lord, 59
Walk Humbly with God, 31

Songs:
Carol of the Child (CD 2, Track 14)
Here I Am (CD 2, Track 9)
I Thirst for You (CD 2, Track 5)
Let Us Go Rejoicing (CD 2, Track 8)

Make Us Worthy (CD 2, Track 11)
Return to the Lord (CD 2, Track 15)
Show Me the Path (CD 1, Track 17)
Take, O Take Me As I Am (CD 1,
    Track 2)
Turn My Heart, O God (CD 1, Track
    20)
Warm the Time of Winter
    (CD 2, Track 10)
We Are Called (CD 1, Track 15)

Word of God

Prayer Celebrations:
I Will Plant My Law, 15
In the Morning Let Us Sing, 43
Let My Prayer Rise to You, 47
Return to the Lord, 59
Walk Humbly with God, 31
You Are Always Near, 27

Songs:
Deep Within (CD 1, Track 4)
Harvest of Justice, The (CD 2, Track 17)
Let Us Go Rejoicing (CD 2, Track 8)
Lord, It is Good (CD 1, Track 14)
Return to the Lord (CD 2, Track 15)
Share Your Bread with the Hungry
    (CD 1, Track 16)
Show Me the Path (CD 1, Track 17)
They Who Do Justice (CD 2, Track 6)
We Are Called (CD 1, Track 15)
We Praise You (Haas) (CD 1, Track 12)

Worry

Prayer Celebrations:
Come and See, 63
Great Joy, 55
I Will Bring You Home, 35
I Will Plant My Law, 15
With You By My Side, 39
You Are Always Near, 27

Songs:
Come and See (CD 2, Track 18)
Deep Within (CD 1, Track 4)
God Is Here (CD 1, Track 1)
Here I Am (CD 2, Track 9)
I Am for You (CD 1, Track 19)
I Thirst for You (CD 2, Track 5)
Return to the Lord (CD 2, Track 15)
Shepherd Me, O God (CD 2, Track 3)
Show Me the Path (CD 1, Track 17)
Turn My Heart, O God (CD 1, Track
    20)
You Are Mine (CD 1, Track 15)
You Will Find Me in Your Heart
    (CD 1, Track 10)
With You By My Side (CD 2, Track 1)

ABOUT THE AUTHOR

DAVID HAAS is the Director of The Emmaus Center for Music, Prayer and Ministry, and Campus Minister/Artist in Residence at Benilde-St. Margaret's High School in St. Louis Park, Minnesota. A composer of over 40 original collections of liturgical music with GIA Publications, he has also authored over 15 books on music, liturgy, religious education, youth ministry, prayer, and spirituality, and he is a monthly columnist for *Ministry and Liturgy* magazine. Haas has been active for many years as a conference and workshop speaker, consultant, concert performer, and recording artist, and also serves as a Senior Advisor for Harcourt Religion Publishers. He has been an active leader in whole community catechesis, and in working with young people all over the world, as founder and executive director of Music Ministry Alive! (a national liturgical music formation program for youth).

NOTES

NOTES

NOTES

NOTES

NOTES

NOTES